Living as I want to

Written and edited by Omar El Bachiri

All rights reserved. No part of this publication may be reproduced, distributed, or transmitted in any form or by any means, including photocopying, recording, or other electronic or mechanical methods, without the prior written permission of the publisher, except in the case of brief quotations embodied in critical reviews and certain other noncommercial uses permitted by copyright law.

2017 Omar El Bachiri El Boudouhi Copyright ©.

ISBN: 978-99920-3-137-7
Legal Deposit: AND.206-2017

First edition: May 2017

Translation: Robert Goitia

Original title: Vivo como Quiero

Omar El Bachiri was born January the 5th of 1977 in Morocco, in a small town of the province of Nador. At the age of two years, he emigrated alongside his family to the Principality of Andorra. Later on he acquired the Andorran nationality. He is licensed in clinic psychology by the Universidad Nacional de Educación a Distancia (UNED).

Writer and editor of the best seller *"Happy and with Savings"* sold in various countries. Among them the United States, United Kingdom, Spain, Andorra and France. Now he surprises us with this new book.

His main passions are practicing sports, traveling and dancing. You can find him anywhere in the world, always with a big smile alongside his wife.

His favorite phrase is: *"I only take care of what I think and say, not of what you understand."*

His motto is: *"Happiness is pure logic. If you are bad and complaint, when you're good, smile right?"*

Also, there is a phrase that it isn't his, but, from a good childhood friend: **Ismael González:**

"Humbleness is a grade you obtain by being fair."

This book is a manual to be checked every time you lose track of your life. Reading the words written in it, you will center yourself again and will be on your way. All are good. Maybe the one you follow today won't be the same that you are interested tomorrow. Its evolution, with each lesson we learn, our preferences and tastes go changing. Not for bad or for worst, only you decide what perspective to take.

Your happiness depends exclusively on you

You are happy by you and for you. All you do, you do it for you. When you do something for someone, you are actually doing it for yourself. You feel better than if you wouldn't do it. You feel the joy that invades you when you do it. So never delegate your happiness in others. You go first, then you and if something is left, is their turn.

When all is good, everyone likes you and hang around with you. Sadly, when you are not doing that well, few remain by your side. Which proofs that first goes your happiness and wellbeing and then comes the rest. Society conditions us to believe that is called selfishness and nothing further from the truth. It's called coherence. Selfish is a person that only looks out for himself even though he has his own needs covered, he doesn't share nothing. This book is about covering your needs and once they are covered, sharing the rest that is left.

Live as you want!

Special thanks to: I want to thank all of my friends and close ones that in a direct and indirect way have contributed to the making of this book. But I want to make special mention to some of them, without them it would have been very difficult to make it. The order of appearance in the names it is neither binding nor significant.

Fanny, Tano, Bego, Oliver, Sinfreu, Naudí, Solsona, Aleix, my mother and father in law (Felipe and Luisa), the girls from bar Cataluña, the public Library of Encamp and my parents.

I start with my partner, **Fanny**, which has contributed with her patience and unconditional love in all of the issues discussed.

Tano, for all of the hours we talked about the ideas in it and giving me his personal perspective. Besides, he has joined me in many of my travels.

Bego, for helping me out with corrections and grammar. I have lunch with her any time I can and there's opportunity.

Oliver, for giving me the idea to write about appearances. We see each other at the gym and there we talk about often about the subject. Why do many people live trying to be what they are not?

Sinfreu, Naudí and Solsona, these three friends, are the base of my theories about investment. We spent hours talking about in what to invest so our money has the best performance possible.

Aleix, that besides being a friend, I also work for him, in his construction company. We talk a lot about happiness and investment having coffee at his mother's bar, *"Bar Lugo"*.

We're both coffee lovers and after a long day of work, we like to sit and discuss about politics and economy.

My in-laws (Felipe and Luisa), have joined me without any interest to all of my presentations for my book *"Happy and with Savings"* and all of the conferences I've given.

The girls at the bar Cataluña, for being so nice and kind when they serve my coffee while we talk about economy issues.

The public Library of Encamp, I am thankful for allowing me to do my book presentations and letting me talk about the issues discussed in it, for giving me the opportunity of being known in a national level. Thanks to it, I am on all types of media in the country.

My parents, I thank them for the education they've given me. Since I was very little they've taught me that it all depends on my way of seeing and understanding situations.

Prologue

The book is divided in two parts.

- I live the life I want.

- I live the life I would like.

- *"Appearances"*

During your reading, I will explain you, to what point your surroundings influence on you. Your past, present and future are included. From which place your doubts and fears come from. Why do you buy or sell any product. Are you one of those that when they hear the word investment escapes running? You may know why.

When you finish reading it, get back on these words and reflect a bit on them. You will see your conduct is very influence on your surroundings.

All of the stories told in the book are based on actual facts. They are people I've known during my travels around the world.

To preserve their anonymity, I've changed their names, jobs and places they live in. Including the main character, even though I speak of it in first person, let it not fool you. It could be either a man or a woman. I don't mention its name in any moment.

Maybe it's your story!

I hope to encourage you to live as you want and if not, that at least this reading distracts you and enjoy it.

First Part

(I live the life I want)

Is about the life you have, with a job you like but in which you are not earning enough to live the life you want. I invite you to follow the guidelines I shape in it, with them you'll learn to earn more. Now, if you are lucky and have a job you like and besides, you earn enough to lead nice kind of life, but you are not living as you want, this is your book.

You'll understand why you don't!

Instead of living as you want, you live as they let you, you'll end up as those people I mention in the second part of this book. Pretending the life you want to lead, with all of the emotional consequences and general discomfort that it leads.

This is the story of two friends from work. One lives according to his beliefs, values and expected pleasures. Likes to travel and going out with friends every now and then. He lives the life he wants. Since he was a child his parents have educated him to be a proactive person. So he can decide for himself how his day is going to go and also, he has been taught very basic values but very efficient ones:

- You come to the world to smile and enjoy to the limit.
- Don't fear death, it's just part of life.
- Saying No, is an option as valid as saying Yes.
- Money is there to give us time, not to enslave us.
- Treat others as we want to be treated.

The other friend, on the other hand is constantly very limited to do what he wants. He barely makes it to pay the rent and monthly costs to live.

He doesn't understand how his friend, earning the same salary as he is and with a very similar life style, can travel so much. On a good day, he decides to ask him. He answers with another question – do you invest? His answer is negative. What is investment? – He asks. His friend amazed says: let's have a drink and I will explain.

- **Investment:** you have a certain amount of money and you buy assets with the hope to regain the totality of that money, plus some added interests. With these interests, you may be able to cost your pleasures. You rather delay an immediate pleasure for a better one, a long term pleasure.

Let me explain you in another way so it's even clearer for you: it's as if you were a moonlighter, it means, you have many jobs but you are not present in them, there are other people working for you, in exchange, they take a small commission from your benefits. You are like the manager of a company and those commissions are the salary of your employees. But before we get going, answer me this question:

- Do you know the difference between liabilities and assets?
- No, I have no idea.

Let me summarize it really fast, liabilities are any product that takes away money from you and assets are the contrary, they are any product that produces money for you. Many people don't distinguish them and fails in investments.

A product can either be a liability or an asset. Learn to distinguish them!

It isn't the same to have a rented space, than an empty one or a home for you to live, than to rent it.

Let me explain you how do I do to live as I want with the salary that we get. You've said it yourself, we earn the same. But before I begin I want to tell you the story of two girls that I met in Tokyo and that got me into investment, Cindy and Jessica, we met singing in a Karaoke, and they are from Chicago.

Cindy: she works in education; she is a math teacher in an institute in Chicago. She wasn't always a teacher, at first; she was a fund manager of high risk investment in the central bank of the same city.

Her dream was always to dedicate herself to teaching but when she finished it, she had to return the loan acquired with the bank to pay for such studies. In United States is very expensive to study a career in the university, young adults get themselves in huge debts so they can pay a career.

She wanted to be a math teacher but the salary was lower than what she earned in the bank. As a teacher, the salary is 1.500 dollars and as a fund manager she earned 2.000 dollars. These 500$ were the payment for her rent. The life as a fund manager was good, but it didn't fill her, she was missing something.

After a lot of meditation, she made a few good investments for her clients and in only 5 years she earned 60.000$ in commissions, and with the 40.000$ she had in savings, she bought an apartment and now, she doesn't need to pay rent, she left her job in the bank so she could get the job she actually wanted. She finally was living the life she wanted. She can say she lives the life she wants.

Jessica: she is a fitness trainer and she loves her work, she was living a nice life but she wanted to move to a bigger apartment because was going to be a mom and hers, had only one bedroom and it was too small for her. The only problem was the rent price. That's where the dilemma started, returning back to her old job in accounting, where she earned more or not moving. Those 100$ of difference had the fault.

Cindy advised her and she invested her money with her. She had 15.000$ in a savings account that barely reported a 0,8% in interest rates annually. She invested it in a fund that reported annually 10% earnings. That's like 1.500$ a year, divided by twelve months, is 125$.

She could move and live as she wants. No need to quit her job. Now she is still working in the same gym and her daughter has a room for herself.

- But these interests gain are too high to be true, I find it hard to believe. I can barely get a 0,5%.

- Let's see, if you don't financial or emotional intelligence, you will never get it. Most of you settle for that 0,5% or as much, with a 1,5% annually. That means nothing. When you acquire this knowledge and enter the world of finances you discover that there are a lot of more options.

In all of the stories I am going to tell you, their leading characters have invested in investment funds and shares. In which they've started questioning its future and deciding on it, they have prepared for it meticulously.

They visualized themselves 10 years in the future and they saw and imagined the life they wanted. They visualized a project, a purpose in life, a motivation to do things and get up each morning joyful and smiling. They drew a road towards success. They've started with long term deposits to get used to banking terms, like fixed and variable income, like other more.

They acquired the habit to go to the bank at least, once a week.

- Once a week, for what? If I can do the papers on the Internet.
- We move by emotions, good or bad ones. The other person that is in front of the counter has and feels emotions toward you. If you want to acquire and practice emotional and financial intelligence, you'll have to practice.

What better place to so than in the bank? It's ok that you want to do the papers from home. I also do so, but that doesn't forbid me from going at least one day a week to visit that bank employees. Business is contact with others, it's interaction between people.

Don't forget!

To get familiar with investment and gain confidence in yourself, you must start from zero and there you can learn a lot. It's the base, once you know the subject and do your own investments, you'll go with less frequency to the bank. But personally, I recommend going once a week.

Worry about your money!

One thing must be clear, money is emotional. It doesn't exist as such. If you don't have a need or an emotion, you won't spend, for as much as you have. If you got 50 €, but you don't want nothing, you won't spend. But, if at a certain point you go into a bar and your soccer team is playing and scores, you may be able to invite your friends a round of drinks.

I go on with my story. They've invested time and money. In their free time, instead of staying home on the couch watching TV, they've used that precious time to educate themselves financially and emotionally.

Also, when they saw TV, it wasn't to see trash TV, but economy and culture shows. They understand that television is an entertainment object, to spend a nice time. Its fiction is not reality. This is out there, on the streets, with friends and family. If you see it to evade your reality, you are going to have a really bad time because you are going to believe everything they say on it. To run away from reality for a while there more healthier options, for example: doing sports, going out or reading. Find for something to do and that gives you a mental and physical benefit.

Your body will thank you for it!

Don't allow that in your mind enters information that makes you dumb and distracts you from your objective, economical independence, or at least, acquire certain financial freedom. I will explain more on the subject furthermore but first, I will explain you what is aversion to take risks. It's a very important factor in any investment you are going to do.

Aversion to risks: the preference for a product even though its costs effectiveness is less but with minor risks than one with better costs effectiveness but with higher risks. I shall explain with a metaphor.

The corridor: there are two races, one of 10 km and the other of 20 km. The registration for both of them costs 35 € and the prize is 70 € for the short one and 120 € for the long one.

According to your physical condition, you'll opt for one or the other. In your case, according to your financial intelligence you'll choose one option or the other.

But choose one, don't leave your money without costs effectiveness.

Why do you think the bank offers you that tiny interest rate? It's very easy for them to do it.
Both of these knowledges are very important if you don't want to end up like many other people which have ended up ruined. You can't enter into the world of investment blinded, just because many other people did it. You won't win the biking regional championship if you don't know how to ride a bike, right? As good as you are running, swimming or skiing, if you don't know how to ride a bike, it's impossible that you can even make it to the goal.

Emotional intelligence: knowing your own emotions and feelings to verbalize them and manage them adequately. Being conscious at any moment of what is going on around us. Knowing your own limits to know to see how far you get. Having the capacity to empathize with others, putting yourself in their place and recognizing their needs to satisfy. This ability is fundamental to stablish social relationships and personal links with others. Besides, in the world of business, you add the capacity to not lead yourself by emotions. But an important facet of this intelligence is its action triad:

Action triad: *I want something. I can't. I do it.*

On this triad it's very important to follow the established order, an alteration of the order of these factors, alters the product.

Against any objective you set yourself, first comes to mind: I want to do it but by certain circumstances of life I can't do it. There's where the action ends. Mistake.

It has to be, I want to do it but by certain circumstances of life, I can't. This is basically the same, but now comes: I can't right now. Now, what can I do to achieve it?

This is the question you have to ask yourself. When you have the answer, do it. *The "I can't" is always temporary and not definite.* It's the motivation to act. Acquire that as a way of thinking!

"Don't limit yourself and don't put stones on your own road"

Example: I want to go on vacations to this place but I don't have enough money. That means I can't. I ask myself: What can I do to achieve that amount of money and go on vacations? When I have the answer, I act accordingly and I go on vacations.

As I mention before, money is emotional. If you live in distress, scared, waiting for the worst. The amount of money that you handle is a reflection of your mind, of your thoughts. It is of vital importance to have an attitude of steel and to know how to manage emotional states, joy and sadness. It's fundamental to strengthen the Resilience.

Resilience: it's the capacity to overcome the bad times; it's to come out victorious of them. As bad as life gets at certain point, you move on and go back to be the person you were before. If you were a smiling and joyful person and you've gone through a bad experience, falling in a state of depression or in a state of anxiety. Once you overcome that, you go back to be that same smiling and joyful person you were. You don't allow a bad experience to condition your character.

I will explain it to you with the dock example: it resists very high pressures; it goes shrinking until it turns solid but once it lets the pressure go, it goes back to its natural state.

It's very important to have good mental health and of vital importance in the world of investment, because things don't always turn out as we planned. I give you a guideline of behavior for you to strengthen it:

1- Act with decision, no matter which one you take, accept its consequences.

2- Value what you get instead of yearning for what you lose. On each decision you take, you'll lose or gain something.

3- Bad things are there for you to learn from it and the good things, to improve and/or accept.

4- Set yourself goals and go for them. This will show you new ways of learning to face your future problems.

5- Practice sports and the discipline you get focus it as a lifestyle. This will make you be more disciplined and organized.

A very important part of sports is the spirit of overcoming that you acquire. You learn that in every day of training you can overcome yourself and if you apply this to you way of life, you become someone constant and decided.

You will take life as a challenge and with it, you'll always be motivated to overcome yourself. Having motivation in life is the core and essence of all joys. This can overcome anything.

Financial intelligence: This is the kind of ability that allows a person to find and manage resources to live as he or she wants to. You get habits, manners and knowledge to know how to read and translate economical balances, solve and avoid any economic problem. That's why it's important. That means your way to see and deal with money. Your economical context.

Economical context: let's say it's as big as a glass of water and then you start filling it with liquid, once it's full, it will spill. All the liquid that keeps falling from it will be wasted. You won't be able to keep filling it. You'll have to enlarge the context, change the glass for a bigger recipient. The larger the context more is the money that comes in.

His is what usually happens to people that win the lottery. In no time they go back to be as they were before or even worst, full of debts. That also happens when someone is used to manage a certain amount of money, compared to those who have more; they don't know how to manage it. If you are used to live with 1.000 € a month and then you get a raise to 1.500 €, at first it will go fabulous but after a year, you'll get used to that quantity and when you had 1.000 € you were drowned, with 1.500 € you'll also be. Someone can only manage the amount of money they are used to handle. If you expand your mental context, you'll know how to handle larger quantities.

Our friend Carlos, now that is manager and earns more than before, must get really relaxed till the end of the month.

And how does he get? Fatal as always. He used to earn 1.200 € and now he gets 1.600 €. His mentality is to waste and his money burns in his hands. He doesn't know another way of life and thinks it's common to have debts.

Another curious thing about money: if you receive a high amount of it from all of a sudden, at first, you'll be very excited but after two or three months, you go back to the same old mood. If you were sad or bitter, you go back to that same stage. With a better car or house, but you go back to your previous stage. This doesn't change people; it feeds what they already are. That typical phrase: money changes people, is not true. It encourages them!

That people have always been like that. In a minor measure but they've always been like that.

The two factors that are more important and you have to take into account before starting any new investment is:

- Why do you want to invest?
- What do you want to do with the money you earn?

It's essential to know the motives; you must know your motivation. If you don't have the right motivation you'll soon stop doing it. Is like going into a diet: you set yourself to lose some pounds, you make sure you eat the right things and you choose the exercises that benefit you most. If you don't know how many pounds you want to lose. You won't even know what to eat, or what exercises to do. Well, when you invest, if you don't know how much money you want to earn or in what you are going to spend it, you won't achieve anything.

By the way:

- What kind of mentality do you have, of a rich person or of a poor one?
- I don't understand. What is that?

The mind of a poor person is that you depend solely of what you earn from your job. On the other hand, the mind of a rich person is that beside what you earn from your job, you have other ways of income.

I have the mind of a rich person. Besides what I earn from my current job, I have many other ways of income. These sources are my assets. I like to invest in bank products.

- So, do I have the mind of a poor person, no?
- Right, you are getting it.

Now that you understand this, ask yourself: how is it that you are not living the life you want.

- Are you a tree? I would say no. You have use of reason and the capacity of decision, which means, free will. No one is holding you back in your comfort zone and forbidding you to progress. The trees, only ask for water and sun not to die. Do you only want not to die? Or on the contrary, do you want to live as you wish?

Move!

- It's just that I love my job. I got good friends there and I have a good time there although I don't earn enough to live as I would like to, it does to live a pleasant life.

I don't want to quit it for another one that's better paid; I have really flexible schedules that allow me to enjoy free time. Once I was asked for what did I worked for and why did I accepted this job and I answered: to have free time once my workday was finished and because I liked it. I am passionate about what I do.

-You've just defined happiness. Being happy, is that very same thing. Doing what you like to do. Complaining less and acting more, being thankful with what you have and value it.

You are someone that when you don't like something, you say it. You complaint, but only once. The second time, you act and if you don't, you adapt and shut up. You know that complaining more times it's useless; it only creates a bad environment in your circle. Congratulations, you are happy and enjoying it. This state of happiness is kept by two independent values: **thankfulness and attitude.**

Thankfulness: Being conscious of what you have and taste it. Take nothing for granted, what you have today, maybe tomorrow you won't have it. While you have, you enjoy it until you are satisfied.

Attitude: Your way of understanding and living life. It's divided in two ways, the positive and the negative. This creates your reality, only you can decide if it's good or bad. It if affects you or it doesn't. Focus on what you have and not in what you are missing. What you are missing has to become the motivation to acquire it and not in discomfort because you don't have it. It's the most important of these two values, because it allows you to control yourself before any situation.

I congratulate you, because you already have what any person is looking for. That's what all investments are about, working in what you like even though you are not earning enough to live the life you want, but you may be able to earn money through other sources to compensate that lack of income. This way you'll always be happy. You'll work in what you like and besides, it will cover your pleasure needs.

Being happy is not a right or an option. It's a fact. It's simply feeling happy with one self. Being happy or sad, if at that point you're fully conscious of it, you are happy. You know that's a fleeting moment and you'll come out reinforce.
If you are sad, you'll know what you're not supposed to do to fall down again. And if you are happy, you'll know what to do to repeat it. It's said is a choice because is the most logic way to act.

There's nothing better than feeling good!

- Hey, this seems interesting. I like the way you present it. It seems fun and entertaining. It sounds to me like stock market, right?

- On one side, but is not just to invest in stock market. As I mentioned before, is to deposit your money in a place, it can be in the bank, in properties, raw material like gold and silver. It's very diverse.

Now I go into details and I will explain it better to you. What's important is that you like it and that you feel comfortable doing it. In my case, is bank investment. I love this system and above all, I love credit cards. I love to pay without having money on me.

Being at home and paying a plane ticket to anywhere in the world. Buying what I want and paying the next month without any interests.

I am going to tell you how I've done this. As I said before, it all depends on your attitude. In my case, crisis made me react and invest. On yours, is the contrary. You just settle for it and accepted your new financial situation. All crisis is a chance to improve and/or change behavior habits.

Personally, I've always liked challenges and this was one. Having financial freedom before turning 65 years old. Between salary decreases and social cuts, each time we were poorer.

In this five years our salary has decreased 20% and taxes have been raised another 12%.

I wanted to maintain the same life level without having to stop traveling I had to do something. Or change my job to one that paid better or invest to regain that 32%. You already know my academicals and professional preparation. If I'd have wanted I would be working for the competition, with a better salary, but I didn't want to. I like my job, for the same motives as you. I am also happy, just like you. I don't complain about my misfortunes, they come up for us to learn from them and come out reinforced. If I don't like something, I act. I don't stay there waiting for someone to solve it for me. Each time I encounter an obstacle, I consider is for me to learn from it and redefine my way to success.

I suppose that as conscious person that you are you are already saving part of your income for your retirement. I personally save 20% of my income monthly.

I'm going to explain you how I did it. First, I saved for a few months and when I had 1.000 €, I invested them in an investment fund that gave me 8$ annually, those were 80 € to my benefit. My money was already working for me. I had the option to invest in stock market and earn a bit more but at that time my aversion to risk was very high.

I started bit by bit; my first goal was to earn to cover my annual passive expenses. Later on, the monthly ones, without counting my home and while I got more knowledge, the more risks I took. Now, after 18 years of investment, I can finally cost my way of life. My assets allow me to lead the life I want, the bars, parking and bank investments.

What I get paid in my work I transfer it totally to my parents; they've had a tough life and haven't been able to save money. With the retirement pay they get from the government, it barely does to pay the rent of the house. Anyhow, in their times, there wasn't that much information about investments. It was a very different time and people believed that to earn money, you just had to work hard and live the day. This is why you work so much. At that time, leisure was inexistent. It's not like now a days, that after a workday you can do anything you want. Go to the movies, gym and theater; go out with the friends, etc. Besides, the government had promised them a deserving retirement pay if monthly they were quoting certain amount in social insurance and hasn't been like that.

See the difference between you and me? You have settle with the salary decrease and the tax raise but me, I've acted and I've learned how to take advantage of a bad time to make it into something good. If it weren't for the crisis, surely, I would still depend solely on my salary.

I don't complaint much and I assume my responsabilities!

On the banking area there's basically three products: the assets, the funds of investment and the deposits. There's a lot more, but they are already derived from these. The assets are the ones that give you the bigger benefit and the deposits the ones that give you less.
The funs of investment are between both. I am not going into the definition of each one because this book is not about financial products. I advise you to go to your bank and inform yourself of the advantages and inconveniencies of each one.

Something I can assure you is that you'll make the most of your money than leaving it in the bank account.
With the assets you take the risk to lose everything invested instead with deposits, you don't. It's what the rule of investments says:

"The bigger the risk better is the benefit". This works for any investment you do. But before I go on, I'm going to explain you the three questions that you have to do to yourself before you begin any investment.

1. Why do you invest?
2. How much money are you willing to lose?
3. Do you take into account the three values?

First question: Why do I want to invest?

- Wait, he says to his friend interrupting him, why don't you ask yourself instead, why invest? Instead of why do you invest?
- No my friend, if you ask yourself why invest? The possible answers are, because many people do it and it works out for them and because the media says so. It's odd but people only tell you the story of their earnings with their investments, they never mention their lost. Instead, if you ask yourself why do you invest? You open your mind to other ways of earning money. You free yourself from prejudices and you come out of the social cell, where it's believed that you can only earn money being present and/or doing many hours.

You are setting yourself many other ways of thinking. You begin to plan your way of life. To live as you want. You break the chains, you free yourself from acquired thoughts and you become free, becoming someone with motives to realize his goals and not with excuses, to not achieve them. But be careful, earning money without you being present is very juicy and greedy. This is very powerful, it can make you live the life you desire or it can ruin you. Inform yourself of how to use it in your favor.

You intend to earn enough for a trip, car insurance, the gym quote, annual taxes and any other expense you want. Picture yourself that people that's every day at least 8 hours in a job they don't like. They simply have it to pay debts generated leading a life they don't desire. Isn't it curious?

They enslave themselves with a lifestyle and rhythm of life they don't desire. Yet they defend it with teeth and nails.

And when you ask them why they don't change it to a better one, their answers are always the same:

- It's close to home.
- Better the devil you know than the devil you don't.
- Buff! Having to start again, so boring.

If you don't have the same luck as I and you are in a job that you don't like and besides that you don't earn enough to live as you want. QUIT IT. It doesn't make any sense that you are still in it, let's say you accept it in your 20's and at your 30's you are still in it. What motivation do you have to progress?
Surely you haven't got a raised in these last 10 years. Something is not working; you'll become a negative person or worst, a toxic person. If you're already one of those people, get away from those who want to advance, your negativity will harm them. If you're not going to get up on their flight, make space and let them fly.

They want to fly really high. From up everything seems clearer and with perspective. If you're not of help, don't be an obstacle.

Not worrying about your money is like throwing stones in the orchard and expecting to collect lettuce

Negative people: are people that see the world as a dangerous place and as a place that there's nothing worth enjoying. If there's a sunny day and a cloud appears, they'll notice the cloud and they'll start to complaint and predict there will be rain. They think they know the future; they go ahead of any fact. If today is a bad day, tomorrow will also be one. They search for happiness as a casualty; they think if they're patient and don't do evil deeds, happiness will appear out of nowhere the next day, in any place. They don't know that happiness is a way of life, a way, not a destiny.

Their favorite phrase is: **everything happens for a reason, if I don't have this or that is because is not my time yet.**

They think and act without any evil, but their mood is contagious in a very fast way. They don't realize that their attitude determines their behavior and way of life. For as much as you insist on telling them that the world is wonderful, they won't believe you. If you enter their game, it will be really hard to come out. Besides, they suck on your energy. When you are with them you won't realize it but as soon as you go, you'll find yourself tired and unmotivated.
I will show you some characteristics they have so you can recognize them and get away from them or at least, ignore their commentaries.

- They worry too much about things that can't be change.
- The past is their guide, they live the present accordingly. They are incapable of changing nothing, for fear of suffering.
- They won't come out of their comfort zone.
- As soon as their plans change they complicate themselves a bit and quit.
- They take life too seriously and are unable to laugh at themselves.
- They center themselves only in their weaknesses.
- They care too much about what people might think of them. When actually no one cares, well their lives are quite sad.
- They hold grudges; they will put in your face any situation that has made them uncomfortable even after a really long time.
- They don't plan their life; they just go with whatever happens.
- They don't know that a person with plans is worth two.

If you can get away from them, I give you two guidelines so you can interact with them without being harm by their commentaries, since they won't listen to you then don't let them harm you:
Let them be right all the time and make too much out of the situation. Your life or personal situation has to be always worse than theirs. With these ways of answering, they'll leave you alone when they see they can't influence on you because your life is way sadder than theirs.

According to their favorite phrase, it would be better to say: **everything happens for a reason.** The reason is the consequence of your actions and the reason is to learn from it. It makes you move. It's optimistic.
Why? is a cause. This happens to me for doing it or not doing it.
For what? Is a reason. This happens to me to do it or not to.
After the "why?" always comes the "for what?"...

For example: I've been fired from work because I've arrived late many times. On my next job I won't arrive late. This is why it has happened. So you can learn the lesson!

Change your vocabulary and your perception of the facts will change

Toxic people: in counterpart, these are very evil people. *"Dangerous people"*. Besides sharing the same characteristics than the negative ones, they spent time criticizing others and each other. If they're with you, they criticize others and when you are not there, they criticize you. They like to do evil deeds, they only know that way of life. They live comfortably and without taking risks, they don't want to make an effort. They neither have discipline or determination, they settle with what they have, even though they're not satisfied with it. They complain all the time but they don't do nothing to change the situation. They're envious and liars, feeling inferior to everyone else, they criticize them in order to put them down and feel they are above them. No matter what you do, they will despise it.

They constantly compare themselves with everyone else, only to make clear they are better than them. They try to discourage in everything you undertake. Even though sometimes they don't say it with words, their body can't hide it. Their gestures and looks are affirming it; they are the reflection of their evilness. They judge telling you things that are true and that's for your own good, but oddly they only see your defects.

It's hard to get away from them, they're everywhere. They can be your parents, family, friends, work partners, etc. They usually think that the care they received as children weren't enough to make up for it; they look unceasingly for more attention from others in their adult age. They get it manipulating others, which leave a great emptiness inside. They feel frustrated and abandoned and that sensation leads them to an impulsive and desperate behavior. That's why; you must always do what you like and makes you feel good. If you are wrong, at least you'd enjoyed.

There are two phrases that characterize them:

1-You can't and you know I'm right. They think they can read your mind. It's a very dangerous affirmation if you believe it. It will lead you to quit even before starting anything. Never think that you can't, your mind will believe and will focus on it. It will block and make you stop looking. Instead, think: What can I do to get it? And your mind will start looking for possible solutions and your creativity will dissipate.

2-The richest is not the one that has the most, but, the one that needs less. The meaning of richness is to have more than your neighbor. The more you have, the richer you are. Now, either you're happy or unhappy is another thing. This phrase has been made up by them to discourage anyone that's looking to improve their financial situation. The more you have and are, the more you'll have to offer and give. A part of happiness it's based in sharing what you have with others. If you have to live as you want, the rest you can share it. Never forget that if you don't have, you can't give. Where one eats, two can eat, but three would starve.

Concerning the previous phrase, the right thing to say would be: **Is not happier the one who has more, but the one who needs less.** I'll leave you 5 words so you can lead a conversation with these people without giving your personal opinion and their words won't offend you at all. This can end in two ways: they'll just quit on you for being impossible, because you won't listen to them or on the contrary, they consider you someone that knows how to listen and give advice.

1- Aha
2- You see!
3- You'll see!
4- Let me tell you!
5- Be yourself!

Example of conversation: with a friend from work whom you just can't stand but you just have to put up with him. Remember you don't know his intentions; maybe he wants to get information out of you so he can use it against you. You don't know if he's toxic or simply negative and afraid.

- I've heard rumors that they're going to reduce the roster and is very probable that you'll be one of them.
- You: You see!
- He/She: No, really, I've heard it from a good source.
- You: Aha.
- He/She: I am afraid what if we both get fired, what do I do?
- You: Be yourself!
- He/She: What do you mean by that, should I start looking for work?
- You: Let me tell you!
- He/She: Then, what do I do, should I ask for the bill now or should I wait and see what happens?
- You: You'll see.

This way you'll be able to follow the conversation. With these people you must be very careful with what you say. Your goal is for them to leave you alone and you'll achieve it the diplomatic way and with good manners. Moreover, I'll leave you 4 signs of a toxic environment so you know if you work in one and so you can behave as such.

- Teamwork does not exist.
- Poorly capacitated people get promotions (cronyism).
- There's no plan of work (the job of each one isn't specified)
- When there's a problem, they search for the guilty and not the causes.

The relationship between them is unavoidable and direct. In consequence it affects the company and the worker. Since there's no teamwork, there's no confidence between work partners and even less confidence with the management. Here's where the jealousy and the gossip starts and the environment becomes hostile and distrustful.

When you get a promotion for cronyism and not for capacity the motivation to overcome gets destroy. You don't find sense in improving, which, you do the minimum to justify your place. Since you don't ascend by capacities, the person that's in charge is an incompetent and doesn't know how to manage his or her new position of responsibility. They have no work plan, they don't specify to anyone their role in the company.
This way, every time there's a problem not knowing how to do his or her job, instead of looking for solutions and trying to find reasons so it won't repeat again, they search for the guilty and this way buries the problem immediately. They don't know that maybe the problem comes from ambiguous information they give to the employees. The important thing for this person is to justify his or her position.

I am going to tell you an anecdote that I had with a toxic person: I told him what I did to make extra money and he answered:

- If it's now with the sweat of my forehead, I don't want the money. It's the only way to earn a wage.
- I answered, I practice sports daily. I sweat a lot and I can't get a penny. So this theory is dislodged and if you don't believe me, get a peak a shovel and go dig in the desert and see what you earn?

The cause of not leading the life you desire is not lack of money, but abundance of fear. You rather survive than live. You think you have reincarnation guaranteed and you'll live it the next life. If you believe in reincarnation, perfect. But if you don't, move.

You do it for two possible causes: Unconsciously, you let yourself be led by society or to make believe you lead a life you desire. You realize that you're not satisfied and try to fill that emptiness with objects and ways of acting that really are indifferent to you.

You are like the person that always has the fridge full to not see it empty in the end and the food expires.
As he has been raised in a big family, his parents always had the fridge full. But in his case, there are not many and he does the same. He has the fridge full because it's weird for him to see it half full.
I'll tell you the advantages of being optimistic:

Positive and optimistic people: these are totally different people even though we live in the same world. Just that in any situation in life, they see the positive side. They know what will favor them. Every situation has two parts, the good and the bad. When one chooses the bad one, they must already know the result:

Complaints, anger, discomfort and incapacity to do anything. First of all they're realistic, but they are smart optimistic. That means, they don't think: I've lost my job, I'm going to be optimistic and smile, I'm sure everything will be all right. No.

When a situation like that appears, they it's a problem but they also know that if they do their part, it will get better. They'll look to know, for what? Has happened this situation. The Why? They already know it or can imagine it and once they know the answer they move in consequence. They are people that take control of their life; they know that luck appears when you are prepared and ready to receive it. It passes every day in front of us.

I will tell you a story so you can understand it better:

- **The luck:** Javier, was looking for work as a plumber and every morning he read the diary with the hope to find something, but as he only search as a plumber, he dismissed any other ad that had nothing to do with that job. Right in the foot of the page there was one searching for a waiter.
James, that also was looking for work, notice the ad and paid attention to it and was interested in it, unlike Javier, he was open to anything. On his way to the job interview he found a prized lottery ticket prized with 5.000 €. As you see luck was there for both of them, but only one of them was prepared and ready for it.

I'll explain you the way of thinking of positive people and I will expose some of their characteristics so you can recognize them. They don't understand another way of life other than being happy. They also suffer kickbacks and difficult situations and they're conscious of it. Even though they're going through a bad moment, they are happy; they know it's only temporary. You can be happy and have a toothache. It's not incompatible.

They know that if they say they're doing badly, the day they really be bad what will they say?

I go on with their characteristics:

- They smile a lot; they know that not doing it is wasting time.
- They don't anticipate events; it's not all about them.
- They don't hold on to the past; they know it happened for something and they learn from it.
- They plan for the future but they don't forget the present, they live it to the full, they are open to setbacks.
- They don't take anything for granted, they're thankful, they know that what they have they can lose it or it can change, nothing is eternal.
- They assume total responsibility for their actions; they know that if they don't act, they won't get anything.
- hey know perfection doesn't exist. They do it the best possible, but without obsessing themselves.
- They don't compare themselves with others and if they do it, is to improve themselves, not to compete against anyone.
- They celebrate any day without justification.
- They know life isn't fair or perfect, it's simply life. No one has ever said it was.
- They know it's good to wake up envy, it means you are going in the right way.
- They're responsible for what they think and say, not of what others understand.
- They take nothing personal, not everything bad goes against them.

Now that you know the differences between these people, I will tell you the story of Eva.

Influence on Eva: wants to travel around Europe for three months and she tells it among her friends and work partners.

-The toxic ones tell her: you are crazy a girl can travel all by herself. You'll be raped and robbed. Come on, you'll expose yourself to the worst experiences. What if you lose the passport? What if you get sick? And if you get kidnapped? And if you run out of money? And all possible ifs you can imagine.

-The negatives ones tell her: For what do you want to travel? Why expose yourself to unnecessary risks? Why don't you go with someone? Save money for the future.

-The positive ones tell her: Good idea, this way you'll have new experiences. Very good, a brave girl. Well done, get to know the world and this way you can value your personal situation.

If you get lost, you can always pick up a taxi to take you to the place you are staying.
According to whom Eva listens to, she'll travel or not, if she decides to leave, she'll go with or without fear. With these descriptions I want you to know that your words define your future. Watch out and take care of your surroundings, we are what we say and what we say comes from what we think.

Examine and analyze your internal dialogue. Words become facts. This is why it's important to watch out for who you are with, because of the influence they can do on you.

Maybe you have a great potential in the world of investments and because you hang around with the wrong people you may never develop it.

As soon as you decide to invest, surround yourself with people that also do. Acquire both financial and emotional knowledge.

You can get it through related magazines, newspapers and videos. Later on you can assist seminars. Watch out for your circle of friends.

Don't just let anyone enter!

The story of **John and Tina** comes to my mind: a couple of rockers I met in Memphis. We met in a music bar, he was the guitarist and she was the singer, I got close to the stage to put a few dollars in the tip bucket and Tina invited me to join them for a dance. We dance a couple of songs and we sat in the bar while they took a 20 minutes break.

We started talking about music, what I was doing there, one thing led to another and we ended up talking about their life. They told me they were living their dream, they lived as they wanted.
They are from New Orleans, they had three months traveling around the country playing music and their dream was to do it for the rest of their lives. I asked them that they must earn a lot to live from the music.

- No, John answered me.
- So, how do you do it? I asked him again.
- We got rented parking lots and some assets, with the benefit we get, we pay where we sleep and with what we earn playing, we eat, and we pay our transportation and the taxes of the parking lots. We are delighted.

They were sick of the life they had in New Orleans, they worked at hostels, and both are cooks. They led a nice life, but not the one they wanted. Hostelry is very beautiful, but also much sacrificed. On holidays, while all your friends have the day off, it's when you work the most.

They decided that they had to do something and act, they set themselves an objective. Save up to 100.000 dollar in 13 years and they made it. Before starting, they acquired emotional and financial intelligence. Each time they gathered 10.000$ they bought a parking sport and they rented for 60$. Saving and investing later, they possess 12 parking spots and some cash. With the rent of these parking spots, they get monthly 720$. The cash they invested it in some assets that generate them a monthly benefit of some 50$ extra. That means, they get 770$ in monthly benefits.

They are a great couple; they've invested time and money preparing themselves for the world of finances. They set themselves a goal, they created a road to achieve it and they've made it. It was 13 tough years, but the sacrifice is the price you have to pay to reach your goals.

They are thinking of selling 5 parking spots to buy a local and rent it. If one day they decide to stop traveling, they'll sell all and buy a house.

The best of the story, is that all started by an existential crisis Tina had. She did not find sense to her life. She studied an FP in hostelry thinking she would be happy with her work but as years went by she felt more apathy.

She used to tell herself:

- I am a cook and for that I've studied so much, I am the chef and I should feel great.

Nonetheless, John was aware that no matter how much education we have, we don't have to dedicate ourselves to do what we studied or learned as an office. During the learning we have fun and we have a good time but then, when the time comes to do our work it's not as pretty as before. There are many people that for having a degree in this or that only focus themselves in those occupations or jobs. In the case of Tina, she studied cooking because it was a family tradition. She came from a family dedicate to hostelry.

Existential crisis: it comes when you find no sense to life. You know you're lucky because you're not missing anything, but even so, you feel bad and empty. You can't find the answers to your questions about life:

What are you doing here?
Why have you been born if you die later?
Why are you never happy? And many more of this same style.
You can avoid going through this bad experience if you live as you want. You'll avoid many headaches and frustrations. You won't have to ask yourself these questions because you'll already have the answers. You'll be giving it a sense to your life. Doing what you want!

- And have you always earn in investments?
- Well, when I started, I did it at safe value. Which I always earned something, little, but it was something. Investing and learning each time more, I became a very good friend of failure.

You learn more from it than from triumph. This works for any circumstance in life. When all is going for you, you don't renew, you keep it up with the same thing. This is necessary to learn and improve. You must be very careful with triumph, it can blind you and make you lose track of reality. You become confident, distracted and careless, you stop taking precautions. I'll give you an example so you can understand it better:

Cristina's bar: this girl opened up a bar. She was making hamburgers and sold really delicious beers. Such was the success, that in barely 9 months, she had to hire 5 employees. But the real success of the business was how nice, thoughtful and kind she was with the clients. She always was with a big smile in her face. The business was doing well, but she didn't knew how to handle success and the volume of work was such, that she left aside her clients and focus only in billing.

She barely smiled to her clients and when one asked her for a bit of attention, she answered she had no time to lose. That she had to do burgers. She forgot that the added value of her bar was herself. Her charismatic and kind personality. People went to the bar to see her and talk for a while with her. She had such a positive and joyful energy that was contagious in the environment. When she changed her attitude and became careless with the clients, they stopped going to the bar and went with the competition.

After three months she had to meditate on her attitude, she realized her mistake and started to smile again and enjoy her work, without stressing herself and talking to her clients.

She remembered why and for what? She opened the bar. When you lose track of your investments go back to asking yourself the same questions that led you to invest.

In adversity, qualities awake by need but in commodity are asleep.

It hasn't been easy but it was worth it. The first thing I did once I took the decision to invest was to prepare myself, in emotional intelligence as well as financial intelligence. On the emotional it's very important to control that inner voice that is telling you constantly, watch out, it isn't safe and introduces you fears for you not to act.

In school we are prepared very well academically, but they don't teach anything about how to spend money, invest it or even worst, how taxes work. It's very necessary for the proper performance of a country, so we can enjoy wellness in conditions. If you know its function, it will motivate you to earn more and pay less. From school we come out prepared to work, but for others, to create our own business and be autonomous.

Passive expenses: these are expenses that you have only for breathing, there are annually and monthly.

Annually: the insurance you have hired, taxes, housing community, gym fee, car maintenance, etc.

Monthly: House, electricity, water, food and any hobby you have.

Since I've already talked to you about intelligences:

- Haven't you noticed that society moves by the same pattern?
- Hmm, the same pattern?

Yes, the youth when they start to work, instead of saving and buying assets to live from generated interests, they buy passives and worst of all, they get debts with unnecessary loans. They don't know anything about investments and get mortgaged. According to them, investing isn't safe, and so what's a mortgage?

Many believe that is like going to the shop in town and saying: give me a roll of bread that I will pay it to you later, thinking that if they can't, they can pay it the next day. I am not saying that mortgaging it's bad, on the contrary. It's a good investment, but only if you know the reason why you are doing it.
If it's by fear of not know where you are going to stay after retirement or for a social trend, your destiny is financial ruin.

On this particular case, it's better to have cash that a house. This will never be yours. You are always half ways with the state and/or with the neighbor's community. When you want to do a reform, you'll have to ask permission to the government and also the neighbor's community.
You have to enjoy investments, if you do them for fear. Your mind will focus only on the negative and won't see the opportunities to advance. It will only see the dangers, imaginary ones but he sees them. Call your inner voice so it can take control. You are moved by emotions and not by reason. Forgetting you left them at home when it was time to invest. Never take an important decision when you are too happy or to sad.

You won't think with reason, but, with the emotion of the moment. Maybe there's a chance to sell the house and then you don't do it. Or it isn't worth buying and you do. Also, social trend, you don't know the reason of others to buy.

Maybe, they work in real estate and they do it for you to copy them. You just imagine, but you don't know. I will tell you the story of three business partners:

Juan, Susana and Jose: we met in Amsterdam, having some coffee in one of their famous coffee shops; they were preparing their new sell. They had an online shop. They were from Valencia but were living in Berlin. They sold any product they propose themselves. They were conscious that many people move by jealousy and pretending something they're not. Simply, to not be less than their neighbor and took advantage of that situation.
On that occasion they were pretending to be a marriage and their son. They move to a community area.

Juan pretended to be the father and dedicated himself to the selling of luxury cars. Susana played the mother and her duty was the selling of high couture clothing and Jose was the spoiled son. They bought him whatever he wanted.

They went around town showing off their economic potential and their son, assisted university dressed in the best brands. He dedicated himself to promote the clothing he was wearing among his new circle of friends. All of them were wealthy or at least, they pretended to be. During the first semester of class he had already sold hundreds of pants, shirts and watches. On the other hand, the father had sold 6 Porches and a Ferrari.

The mother, also did her part, she sold 15 dresses from the most prestigious seamstresses at that time. When they managed their objective, they returned to their city to rest and enjoy their achievements. They knew that people simply copy and doesn't ask.

If I have this or that, you'll want the same and you won't ask me what I have done to get it. You'll simply ask me where I have bought it. I'll tell you delighted the place and how to finance it. We live in a society of that consumes similarly like a fast food restaurant: You want something and you get it served in two minutes. This leads to certain consequences. If in that food there's the cholesterol and the fat, in the society, is the continuous lack of satisfaction. You get all at the moment and no one stops to think:

Why have they bought it and for what?

In life you can have it all but not at the same time. The media bombs us with publicity so we don't even have time to think and even less, reason. Copy your neighbor and but the same thing as he does, but above all, don't question it. There's a chance you come to reason and get out of the flock. They buy, buy and buy. Let the chain never stop. In this chain also governments wanted to enter and they teamed up with the banks and real estates.

Through the media they led a brutal campaign against rentals. But don't think for a second that these last ones are our enemies. They're there by and for us, they're under our control. They're a reflection of our society, they move according to our needs. If you do a film and you want it to be seen worldwide, they can help you spread the information.

It all depends on the message that you want to send and above all, of what the rest understands. It isn't fair that they are blamed for all the bad things in our society. Don't be a bum and before believing in advance, use your brain and be a critic. If someone announces that a movie is the best of the century, inform yourself before going to see it and you'll have your own opinion.

What happens is, that governments and banks knew how to manipulate people's mind playing with their illusion and taking advantages of school deficiencies in the matter of financial intelligence. Illusion had done a lot of damage, for not knowing how to manage it.

This fascinates me as such, I take it, and I bought it. People say that I deserve it, so this may be true and I believe it as such.

"You deserve it, buy it"

You see, the governments are manipulated by economical power "multinationals". Imagine that you are the president of your country and you want to pass a law that's good for the people but it goes against certain interests of a multinational.

It will threaten you to with closing and firing all of the employees, let's say there are 3.000. What would you do? You'll surely give in to their petitions.

To get people indebted, as a manipulation strategy they used the emotional aspect, this influentiate in fears, joy and illusion. An excesive fear to retirement and not having where to live was implanted.

"Pensions are in danger and that which will be left for you, it will barely do for you to eat"

As a solution to the problem, it was proposed to mortgage yourself. They used one of the oldest laws to enslave people.

"A self imposed necessity"

In the United States, slavery was abolished in 1865 and in Europe begins around the year 2000. People has mortgage themselves to banks at an average of 30 years. They can no longer decide on their future. A few years back slaves paid for their freedom and now people pay to lose it, to acquire slavery. Curious isn't it?

Self imposed necessity: if you want to enslave someone or shorten their rights, create a problem and at the same time the solution. When they come to beg you for help, give them the solution but in exchange of something. They will give delighted.
You can shorten their social rights acquired base on years of negotiations, without any opposition at all.

On the other side, on a cultural level tv shows were shown that incited ignorance and mediocrity was accepted. It was promoted to the audience that it was interesting and it was trendy to be ignorant, misbehaved, vulgar and to not be interested in science.
The socialization, learning and acceptance of these shows induces to conformity, submission, obedience, the acceptance of the social norm and/or dressing according to the fashion standard.

The socialization allows that you feel identified with a group. In this case, the group of ignorant and vulgar people that appear in this shows and the learning is produce with the believes, values, roles and expectations of the group. You'll think that your way of thinking and behaving is conscious, desired and love. But you're actually induced to behave according to a planned strategy, subtly imposed. Every year is more expensive to study an university career, but that doesn't seem to matter to the population.

An ignorant country is easier to manipulate and govern. Don't you think it's strange that daily we only see news of how bad the world is and how dangerous and unsafe it is?

All of these news make you insecure and to stay in your comfort zone. You don't explore beyond that, you know nothing more and believe the world ends there. Traveling as I do, I don't see that much insecurity we get sold in the news.

There's a phrase that says: **"Have the people distracted and you can enslave them and steal from them for as much as you want."**

Governments incentivize consumption with succulent tax benefits, banks gave loans without any conditions at all and real estate companies appeared out of nowhere, in any corner there was one. They first created an inexistent need and then they sold whatever they wanted.

If you didn't have a mortgage, you were no one and besides that, you were unconscious for throwing your money away in rent. Also, it was associated that having a mortgage meant being happy and that's where ecstasy was born. Many young people screamed *I am happy, I have a mortgage!*

The government collected more in taxes, banks gave away loans knowing that people weren't going to be able to pay it back and then they were going to keep those households so they could sell them again, backed by the government. Oddly, when someone asks you for money borrowed and doesn't pay it back, you can't do nothing about it. You lost it. The estate doesn't make the effort for you so you can get it back and they don't even pay it themselves.

But when it comes to them, yes. But the best of all is: you gave them your retirement money!

Another curious thing that makes them special is: they are the only organization authorized to create money out of nowhere. They print as much cash as they want and they decide if the economy is doing good or not. According to their desires. But just like the media, you don't blame them for anything. These are directed by people like you and like me, just that they've acquired emotional and financial intelligence. They play with information that not many people have or don't pay attention to.

At the same time, real estate companies sold any hole as if they were selling gold. It was the offer/demand.
Once their pockets were filled, to justify the current crisis, they blame the citizens. They are told that they have lived above their possibilities and they have created this situation. Caused by their small intellectual capacity and their low performance. They have too much vacations and holidays. They must be reduced and reduce even more wages. To create more jobs. This way, instead of revealing yourself against the system, you blame your closest surroundings and yourself, falling in a great depression.

The people will seem tired and without strength to fight for their rights. They will feel helpless and defenseless with the cuts suffered and will make them even more dependable of the government, if this promises them a better future. It will be even more dependent of the same leaders that have lead them to that situation. Without freedom, there's no action, so that means there's no change.

One, as a citizen trust in the government and in the system of life that this implants and offers. It all goes down to a lack of financial intelligence. In school this should be an obligatory subject. When there's no time to ask these two previous questions, indebtment gets produce: Why and for what have you bought it?

You should've seen that the answers are: to have a mortgage in exchange of losing freedom and because I want to be happy, forgetting that happiness is something internal, not external. Not because you have a house of your own you are going to be happier than living in a rent.

<u>Living has a price, even though is a right</u>

Talking about mortgages, it has come to my mind a couple I met in Bilbao, in their famous museum, during an exhibition of gothic art.

Noemí and Carolina: Was a young married couple from Asturias. They used to work in a supermarket, Noemí was a butcher and Carolina, cashier. They had an 18 year old daughter that was starting university.
Since she was born they've deposited to her 70 € monthly, so when the day came, she could have the money to pay her studies.

They could foresee the future but they weren't able to save 20% of their monthly earning and decided that it was bet to mortgage themselves. They bought an apartment, so when they were retired they wouldn't have to pay a rent and could lead a dignifying life or sell it and with the money they get, leave the rent. When the time comes they would decide. Due to the crisis, they had a little inconvenience with the bank because of the mortgage.

From that moment they lost trust in it and they retired the university savings of their daughter. They invested it in gold. They knew that it was a safe investment and they bought gold ingots. It's not tied to an entity that can go into bankruptcy. Another advantage is that it's money itself and is entirely yours. You don't pay taxes for having it. You can change it for cash at any moment and place in the world. Once a year, when they had the 840 € save they bought ingots.

When Luisa, that's their daughter name, turned 18 years old and wanted to study a career she spoke to her mothers and they sold the gold. They gained a bit more in comparison of the investment they did, it was around 16.500 €. She wanted to study economics and finances, which she understood a lot of investments and interests. She invested the money in a fund which earned her 16% in earnings. With those interests she paid her studies.

A year later, she had 2.640 € to her benefit and could pay her enrollment fee with no need to take out from her savings. She preferred to postpone her studies for a year and obtain a profit from a capital. Once finished, she still possessed the totality of her savings and had the chance to invest it in her life project.

When you invest in gold and you want it to be robbed, tell it to everyone and you'll see how in no time, someone will try to rob it. This is an investment that you have to keep a secret, because you keep it at home.

I've told you this story for you to see the difference mortgage yourself by fear of not having a house to live when you retire and thinking that you won't have to pay more rent you will enjoy your retirement.

The first one incites to anxiety, thinking, if I can't pay my mortgage, I won't have where to live. The second one, instead, invites optimism and motivation to make plans when you retire. With what I save in rent, I can travel, go to the beach, buy presents to my family, etc. As I already said in many occasions, it always depends on your attitude. You decide if you do one thing or the other and how it affects you.

Control your thoughts and you'll control your mind. Control your mind and you'll control your conduct

When it comes to taxes, when a young student gets his first job and negotiates his wage, he remains perplex when he receives his pay sheet. It's lower than what was agreed. He doesn't know that the government keeps a part of it. It becomes your founding partner and capitalist. Starting now, it will be like your couple or travel mate. Of all of which you earn, it will keep a part of it, you will never be apart again. Likewise, it is also of vital importance the influence your parents have on you when it comes to money.

When you lived with them, remember how it was their relationship with it.

They used to tell you phrases like?

- Money doesn't fall from the sky.
- It's dirty, it corrupts people.
- It's not that important.
- As long as you're healthy, why would you want it?
- Only greedy people talk about it.
- Why do you want it? If you can live with a little of it.
- Do you think that I'm a bank?
- Investing is very dangerous, besides, it's a rich people thing.

Sadly, if you've been educated under these teachings, your relationship with can't be good, but don't worry, even if you were educated in this way, if you propose it to yourself and have a steel attitude, you can overcome it and have success in finances.

I'll explain it to you with a metaphor: the same water that rusts an iron bar, it brings shine to a steel one. This proofs that is not the circumstances, but what you are made of. If you are made of iron, water will affect you, but if you are made of steel it will slip on you.

Now that I've brought up the subject of the parents, I'll explain to you a bit the reasons of the education you were given. If you're thankful with your education, perfect.
But if you're not happy with it, but also you're angry at them because they didn't bought you everything you wanted, or didn't gave you the love and attention you wanted, I hope that starting from now you understand and change your opinion about them.

Your parents: first of all, only you decide if something affects you or not. If you want reasons or excuses to act or not. Circumstances and what others do or say doesn't affect you. What affects you is how you understand it. Remember how positive people think: they made themselves responsible of what they think and say but not of what others understand. Apply it to yourself, they're not responsible of what you understand.

Having this clear you can carry on with reading. You've been educated as they knew, how they were taught. They could've taught you their fears and frustrations. If you'd ask them why did they do certain thing or another, they will answer that, that was what they thought had to be done. When they told you not to do this or that, what is bad or dangerous, they didn't do it with bad intention. If they gone through bad times, hunger or fear, with the education you've been given, it was because they didn't want you to go through the same things they did.

They've lived in a different decade than yours, with less technology or freedom of movement. You don't know the situations that they've gone through and how it has affected them. When they didn't bought you the bike you wanted so much, they didn't know how important it was to you. If they know that denial was going to awoke in you so much anger towards them, surely they would have bought it to you.

Remember how you were when you were 10 years old and look at how are now the young kids of that same age. You don't look nothing at all like them. Well, imagine your parents and your grandparents, they look even less like them. Analyze carefully the situation and don't blame them for all your misfortunes.

Instead of focusing yourself in what they didn't gave you, focus yourself in that which they gave you. You'll see it's more than you remember.

They've fed you, dressed and paid for your studies, even though you may think it was their obligation, it was not. As parents, according to the law, they are obliged to not let you starve to death or to die from cold and to enroll you in school. Now think of the food they gave you I really doubt it was just bread and water. The clothes they bought you, surely weren't rags just to cover you from the cold. The school, besides enrolling you, they took you there until you were old enough to go by yourself.

Maybe they haven't attended to any parent meeting, but that doesn't mean they don't care about you. Many parents assist and they don't pay any attention to it, they simply go as mere spectators. There's when it comes the importance of a focusing place that I mentioned before, to maintain your happiness, focus in what you have and not in what you lack. If you blame them for your misfortunes or anyone who is not you, you're leaving your destiny and way of life in the hands of others and that's very sad. You're showing yourself that you have no decision at all about the way your life goes and nothing depends on you.

If you're a parent or one day you want to be one, I give you some advice on education so you see how you can influence in the future of your child. You can guide him or her to be dependable of other, selfish and materialistic (parasite) or on the contrary, to be autonomous, with values and thankful for what he/she has (free).

Having a parasite son/daughter: it's the easiest way to educate. Give him/her everything he/she asks for without asking anything in return. Make him believe he deserves everything, that just by asking for it, he/she gets it.

They have rights but no obligations. They don't need to make any effort to reach the goals they set themselves. To us he is the most handsome or she is the most beautiful in the house, to the rest they'll also be. When they want something and they don't get it, the rest are to blame for not giving it them. They are always right and who doesn't see it like that, is wrong. Don't put them any limit and behave with them as if you were their friend, so the day they get angry at you, they can disrespect you like with any other friend. Spoil them to the extreme, don't let them fall never and above all, don't argue with them.

With this pattern of behavior your son or daughter won't know how to move around the world by themselves. They will always look for approval in others to do anything. When they want something and they don't get it, they'll feel so frustrated they'll opt for being aggressive or submissive; they won't know how to defend their ideas.

Also, if you want to condition their studies so they study with fear of not passing instead of wanting to learn and pass, teach them these fears: tell them constantly that if they don't study or doesn't pass, he'll end up as a homeless person that sleeps on the streets, toothless and smelling bad. Your kids will associate not passing with being homeless or without future at all and will get anxious thinking in the life that awaits them. They'll hate studying, they'll panic, and won't want to know anything about them, and they'll come up with any excuse to not study.

Getting a free son/daughter: talk to them, reason your behavior towards them and ask them for explanations, so that they learn to express themselves and give out their point of view. Set strict limits: If it's white is white, not grey. At home you follow rules and if they don't want to obey them, explain the motives.

Encourage their independence; let them collaborate with home activities: cleaning, ironing and cooking. This way they'll know the effort that means having a cozy and clean home. Explain them the function of money, so he values it. Also, talk to them about dead, so they understand that in any moment either you or they may die. So they don't become dependent of nobody or nothing and enjoy what they do.

This way of educating will mean extra effort from you but in time you'll be thankful. The ideal thing is to start since they start walking, so they see that their behavior has consequences. First of all you are their parent, not their friend. The education of a child is of mutual learning. You also come out stronger.

I go on with college studies, those aren't obligatory. Which means, if you don't have the means to cost them, don't get frustrated or suffer for it. Even though you don't have them, don't pay them entirely, pay a part of it. So they'll value it more. This way you ensure they are studying something they like and not that they're doing them for not working.

The estate gives scholarships, to those who have the necessary grade to access them. They can also work on weekends or holidays. It doesn't matter if they finish their studies later than normal. By normal, I mean the average years stipulated to do so. No one assures them that they're going to find a job once finished their studies or that they're going to set up their own business.

So you see it's not that important, **I'll tell you Emma's case:** she is a 34 year old woman and she is the general attorney of the state of Sofia, Bulgaria. We met in Transylvania, visiting the castle of Count Dracula. We were going in the same tour and during it, we started talking, telling me a little bit of her story. Deserving of admiration. She studied and work at the same time. When she passed the selection at 18 years old, she couldn't go to college because her family didn't have the economical means necessary to cost her studies.

On the other hand, her parents had raised her to be an independent girl that she could move around life without the need to depend on nothing or no one. This is the best heritage we can leave to a child; teach them to be self-dependent. She had really clear ideas; she wanted to be a lawyer since she turned 12.

She got the information of the scholarships the state gave out to students, she made calculations to know how much it cost the lifestyle she wanted to live and she started immediately. The 5 years of studies ascended the 12.500€. Each year costed 2.500€. That's the price for a car. She worked for 4 years to save for them and started working on it. She enrolled herself in the Universidad de Salamanca. In the mornings she went to class and in the afternoon she studied in the library. She worked on weekends, holidays and vacations.

With the scholarship she could afford student residence, with her savings, her studies and with what she earned she lived day by day. She started studying when she was 23 and she got her Law Degree at 28. Many of her classmates finished their studies at around 23, currently they are unemployed. So you see, it doesn't matter the age when you finish them, the important thing is to end them.

Those were 5 tough years, but they were worth it she affirmed, In this case, Emma, didn't want to invest because she didn't want to dedicate time to acquire financial intelligence, her goal was to finish her studies as soon as she could. But she did a huge part of investments, saving and acquiring emotional intelligence.

When you focus in something and you go for it with all your strengths, you get it. At least, that which is up to you. Let's go on with the second question of investment.

The second question is: How much money am I willing to lose?

Because the only sure thing in investments are the losses. You can also earn, that's why you invest. But, like everything, the only sure thing is death. A really important factor to take into account, are emotions. As I already mention before, you leave them at home when it comes to invest. You have to split them from money. Because when you are really happy, you can buy really expensive and when you're sad, you can sell at a really low price. You make the business when you buy not when you sell. You buy cheap to sell expensive.

Even though this rule seems clear, many people ignore it. It's worth for any investment, properties, land, source material, etc. A fisherman buys fish at a price and sells it more expensive, the cheaper he bought it, more is the benefit he gets when he sells it. You must be cold in investments, if you're going to have a bad time, is better for you not to invest. It's like a game, you win or you lose and you must be conscious about it. Ask yourself: what if you lose 10% of the capital?

If you're not going to go through hardships or discomfort, invest. The important thing is to know that you can earn it.

With good emotional and financial intelligence you'll know in what to invest and how.

Third question: do I take into account the three variables?

- Time frame
- Expected rentability
- Assumed risk

- The time frame: is the time you're going to spend before you can retire your money from that product.

- Expected rentability: two important concepts must be clear, fixed rent and variable income.

- **Fixed rent:** you know beforehand the obtained benefit, this can be monthly or annually. In general, it produces less benefit than the variable, but you ensure a safe capital entry, for example: properties and banking products.

Properties: you have a store, a parking lot or a home and you rent it for certain amount of money monthly or annually.

- **Variable income:** in this case it's unknown beforehand the benefit. It depends on diverse factors, like ups and downs of the market. For example: shares of stock, fund of investment or a business of our own. The important thing is to know when money comes in and if you depend on it at that certain moment.

- Assumed risk: is the capacity to confront aversion to risk.

Deciding if it's better to earn something but not losing nothing or in exchange, earning a lot at the risk of losing something. Now that I am mentioning rents, I go back to the case of the young people that mortgage themselves, they skip the third question. Of the three variables:

The time frame, the expected rentability and the assumed risk.

But worst of all is that they can't distinguish between the two rents. Most of them have gotten into variable quotas, that means into variable income, but to the bank. They don't inform themselves in knowing whether they're buying expensive or to a good price, they do it blindly, leaving the possible benefit at random. They don't know when are they going to regain their investment or how much are going to gain or regain at least. You ask them how much have they paid for the square meter and how much would they sell it and they have no idea of what you're talking to them. They believe price is calculated according to the rooms of the house.

Instead of seeking advice by professionals from the financial sector, they do it through family, friends, known people or worst yet, in real estate companies that only want to sell. Is like buying an used car, the seller will tell you is a bargain and is the best buy you can do.
If you want to learn how to play soccer, you won't train with a basketball team. Each one is good in their area. Invest money and time in educating and preparing yourself before acquiring any investment.

This will condition your present and possible future. You go to real estate companies to know about the average price of the market, to the banks to ask for the mortgage and financial advisor to know if mortgage is viable or not. If you want to set up a business, you have to shuffle all of your options. Because if it comes out right, you can live from it, but if it goes wrong, it can ruin you or worst yet, stay indebted for a long time.

You buy merchandise to sell it expecting to regain capital invested more a benefit in the sell. You see, any investment has a risk, either banking, real estate or setting up your own business. Decide which one compensates you more and act. But don't forget taxes, not all products pay the same. As in every country they're different I won't go deeper in the subject.

Talking about business, I've just remembered the story of **Marcos and Lucía:** they were a couple from Madrid that I met in Rio de Janeiro, in the Copacabana beach, they were on their honeymoon. They worked in computing for a big company in the center of Madrid. Their life was nice and they were happy, they had two children. Some friends of Lucia had a restaurant in the coast of Málaga and in a few years they were going to retire and they wanted to transfer it. Marcos always loved hostelry because his parents had a bar outside of Madrid and in one occasion he comment to Lucía that they could open up a restaurant.

This transfer was of 15.000 €. They thought about it really seriously and they calculated the numbers. They educated themselves on how to acquire financial and emotional intelligence and started to save and invest. In this case, emotional intelligence was to leave that money saved and not touch it. It's very curious the fact that having money and it's that when you have some savings, new necessities arise.

They saved up to 300 € each month. When the year ended when they had around 3.600 €, they invested it in a fund of investment that reported them a 9%. In less than four years they saved up the 15.000 €.

They could keep the establishment, they just asked a loan of other 8.000 € to renew it a bit and now they live as they want. The loan they pay it with what they earn in this establishment.

Having financial intelligence, they know the difference between bad debt and good dept. The good one is the one required to invest, you pay it back with what you earn, that means, it pays by itself. The bad one is the one you ask for own consumption that means, you have to pay it for yourself. In Hong Kong, I met a man that said a very interesting phrase:

Change your way of thinking and your world will change

Also, if you want to know the cultural of a person or the environment that surrounds you, asked them about the TV shows they watch and what newspaper they read. In consequence to their answers you'll know what subjects to deal with them and their conducts won't surprise you. You won't have to deal with many arguments, lear to put up with others, you can always lower your cultural level. The day you want something from them, you'll know where to enter.

Knowing this, I change friends. It was one of the best decisions I made in a long time. The environment I was surrounded by did not invite at all to invest, it's very important to know with whom you relate yourself. I drifted away from toxic and negative people and got closer to positive and optimistic people, to see how they looked at the world.

I was sick of listening always the same stories. How bad the world is going and the economy. When I travel, I don't see that, there's everything but above all, I see happy and joyful people.

I couldn't and didn't want to believe that the world was such a sad place and indeed, traveling and knowing other people, places and ways of thinking, I can assure it. The world is wonderful. We have so many reasons to smile and be happy that if I start naming them, I'm afraid I would dedicate three entire books to it. It's wonderful to smile. While you do it, you don't suffer and forget bad times. Is an extreme state of bliss. Imagine smiling daily for at least 4 hours. It doesn't take any effort.

You can do it while you do anything and the best of all, *it's free.*

There's people with a lot of money and doesn't smile. The world is a place full of possibilities to whatever you want. It's made in such way that you can live always happy if you set yourself to it. It hasn't been created to go against you, it wouldn't make any sense. Life is so wonderful, beautiful and simple that explaining it seems complicated and farfetched. Simply, it doesn't make it easy for you, but it has given you intelligence and motivation for you to grow up and live as you want. You have emotions and feel pain so you can decide between what you like and what damages you.

If you follow these 4 laws of nature you'll see it's very simple:

-If it's cold, cover yourself.
-If it's hot, uncover yourself.
-If you want something, ask for it.
-If you don't want something, reject it.

We only have 3 obligations: breathing, feeding ourselves and resting. From there all the rest are preferences

Executing these guidelines, you'll only receive abundance and wellbeing. There are mountains, seas, rivers, deserts, enormous prairies, where the sight can't reach to see the end. If you're born in one place or another, you're limited and conditioned by culture, religion and economy of such place. But you can always emigrate, change of place and beliefs. We are free to act. Those of us who live in the so called first world, we're really fortunate.

It only depends on your attitude in times to confront situations. If you're conscious of this, you may focus in that which you already possess, in material things and as well in the emotional aspect and you'll see how wonderful living is. Be thankful for the simple fact that you're alive and you may take your breakfast each morning.

We have the option to live as we want, that's why I find it strange that there are people that don't do it. We have what we want. We are here for only a while and to be happy. If we lived in a dictatorship, you'd wish to have freedom of movement and thought, nonetheless we live in a democracy and no one acts.

They don't live as they want, but as they're told. Acquiring unnecessary obligations and ways of thinking and acting that are not their own.

Have one thing clear, when someone comes to you with their problems; remember they're theirs, not yours. Is ok to help others, but as soon as it starts to affect you in the smallest thing, turn away.

There's a very curious universal law, called: give to receive.

Give to receive: If you want to receive you'll also got to give, but not at any price, if you don't have, don't give. If you can help, perfect, do it. But if you can't, don't do it. The simple fact of being conscious that you want to help but you don't have the means to do it, it's already enough for you to receive. This law is not as accurate as a boomerang, don't take it so literally. Equally, you only have to give if you want, it's not an obligation. You usually receive half of what you give and is not always like that. It's a statistic and we all know that is the less accurate science that exists. If you have two cars and I have none, according to statistics we have one each. Worst yet, you earn 3.000€ and I earn 1.000€, as the two of us earn 4.000€, statistics say we earn 2.000€ each one.

But is not bad to give a little every now and then, even though it's just to see if the law works

No one comes and says:

-Hey, I'm happy, let's go out to eat, drink something or just goes to you to tell you he is doing great, on the contrary:
-Hey I'm doing badly, lend me some money, they go to you to tell you their hardships and then they go away all relaxed and you have swallowed all of their problems and make them your own, with the discomfort that leads to.

Many people have tried to convince me that you come to the world only to suffer, I pity them but I understand them. They're locked up in a mind cell, they live under, what's known in psychology as *"LEARNT DEFENSELESSNESS"* . I write it in capital letter so you see its importance; it can condition you for life.

Learnt defenselessness: it's related to the condition of a person after having learned passively certain beliefs, convincing themselves that they can't do anything to change their situation.

Your environment goes starting from your family to your neighbor that one you barely say hi to, they can create on you learnt defenselessness. They can draw you with their negativity based on listening and interacting with them. Each time you want to do something different they will forbid it to you with their commentaries. In the long term you'll believe that you can't do anything to change that situation and you'll give up.

I'll give you two examples so you see how it can your environment condition you:

Looking for work: Diego is a young man that's looking for work and each time he has an interview it comes to his mind criticism he receives from his parents and friends. They tell him that he's not prepared for those roles, that they're too much responsibility for him. The fact of giving in and not assist, it gives him discomfort, well he's very hopeful.

He has resigned to look for a job. He has learned that even though he finds it, the day of the interview, he won't go. He has been employed for 2 years, but he has abandoned the idea to look for more, he unable to look for another solution and analyze why he is letting himself be influenced by others. He has accepted the thought that he is not good enough for those positions.

The baker: there used to be a baker in a village that was really sad, he had to sell more cakes or he'll have to close down the business. Most of the inhabitants told him that his cakes were too sweet and discomforted them, that was the reason the people didn't buy them.

One day, he decides to participate in the national pastry contest of the region and to his surprise, he wins it. The board of directors of the contest prize him giving him two more pastry shops, he can place them in any village of the region. The poor man quits on them saying he was just lucky, he recognizes he is a bad baker because he has a pastry shop in his village and is about to broke. They ask him in what village does he have it and he answers that in the last of the region. The board of directors breaks to laugh out loud. What are you laughing about? - the poor man asks, surprised. - Most people in that village were diabetic and are forbidden to eat sweets, they answer.

Don't just let anyone judge you. Before you feel bad about it, analyze the environment that's surrounding you

No one can tell you that you aren't worth it, not even yourself. Maybe you are not good at certain things, but I doubt that you aren't good at something. We all have to be good in something, **look for it!**

You don't know if you're being judged for your own good or on the contrary, they do it for jealousy and want to hurt you.

As I was interested in banking products, I decided to become an expert in them; I read magazines, newspapers and books. I saw videos about economy on internet and I went to different seminars to end up becoming in the expert I am today. I took full advantage of internet, we have valuable information in our hands and for free. That's why it's important emotional and financial intelligence. If you don't have them, you won't pay attention to this information, is like listening to a song in a foreign language, you like it but you have no idea what the lyrics means.

I stopped going to the bank just to know the status of my account and I started to educate myself about these products. I asked about any subject related to them and if something wasn't clear to me, I insisted until I understood it. The bank and insurance agencies, are like a bar, you've got to go calm without any rush. You want your lunch to do good on you, the investments and insurance that you hire, you also want them to respond to you in a good way.

Since I've already mentioned insurance agencies, are another way of investment, not to earn money but they allow you to spend less, which is almost the same. I hire a private insurance so it could cover the part that doesn't cover social insurance. At that time my only income was my salary, if I got sick and couldn't work, that month I was going to get paid less and I couldn't afford that.

Even though the monthly or annual quota may seem elevated, it isn't actually, when you go to the doctor, dentist, hospital, etc., the bill it's usually high and having that insurance, you compensate that expense, it balances it for you. Have your medical needs covered and don't skimp on them.

"A sick organism it's not productive or profitable"

You know what's the only thing a person from a poor country envies from a person of a rich country? Their healthiness. In rich countries, we all have access to it. I could see it myself when I was in India, in New Delhi. There, I met **Aryam.**

I used to have breakfast in his food stand. Since he used to see me there, we created a friendship and told me a bit about his life. He had lived and worked in Barcelona for 15 years.

Saving and investing, he saved some money and he returned to his hometown. He put up his food stand and he lives from it. He lives as he wants.

Some observations he did, got me thinking:

- How can it be that in Europe, having access to public health, there are people with rotten teeth or worst yet, toothless? Also, people suffer from depression and anxiety in really high levels.

- Regarding the first question, it's by two reasons I answered, is it because they have problems with the gums and that makes them rotten or because they rather spend the money in material things, to pretend something they're not. But that's a subject I'm going to deal with later on: appearances.

Regarding the second question, it's a very delicate subject. Our society tells us to go inside a vicious circle, very dangerous and contagious; they want to infuse an artificial happiness.

"I am happy with what I am being sold and not with what I am"

In counterpart, when you already have certain object and you think you're happy, a new one comes out and makes you believe again that you're not, to not be what you acquire. It's the fish that bites the tail.

In poor countries, people fight to survive, which has other social values and don't have time for these kinds of mental disorders. They are conscious that they don't have tomorrow assured, so they live in the present.

In first world countries, since all our basic needs are covered, we look how to fill the spare time we have. It's believed tomorrow is assured. Like today I'm alive, why wouldn't I be alive tomorrow?

When people have time and don't make the best of it to do something productive, they get bored. They start to worry about things that have no importance, spinning their head around it and they end up desiring what they don't have and yearning for what's lost. Since I've already mentioned tomorrow, I continue on with death.

Death: it's unavoidable; it reminds us that we are alive. We should really think more about it, but in a positive way. It's a countercurrent race, against life. If you know you're going to die, why don't you do what makes you happy? If it's because of what others will say, let me remind you that in the tomb or in the incinerator you're the one who is going to be there, not others. No one has the right or the authority to judge you. Only justice can do it and we created it ourselves. To have certain guidelines of acceptable behavior. If you obey them, do whatever you like.

Talking about justice, I've remembered Marta's case, a girl I met in Tampere, is a beautiful city in Finland. She was the town sheriff's daughter. She had a body issue that made her feel complexed; she was overweight because of thyroids problems.

Marta: was 23 years old. In the summer, all of her friends went to the pool but she, stayed in the bar terrace, watching as others bathe and had a great time. We met in that same bar, I asked her why wasn't she bathing with her friends and she answered that she didn't like to wear a bathing suit. Speaking in detail, I saw that her real problem was what others might think of her body. It was a city I loved and I stayed there for 5 weeks. I decided to help her with her irrationals beliefs and negative thoughts about herself.

Based on asking her, why was so important what others thought of her and also a nice cognitive behavioral therapy, she could bathe without any more fears. She involved in it a lot and she advanced at it in a flashing rhythm.

When you think about the actual possibility of dying, many problems you have, aren't that important. Also, if you go to that extreme, you've got to ask yourself:

- In what benefits me the opinion of others? Either good or bad opinion.
- If we listen to that opinion, will we feel better?
- Whom should I listen to, those who give a bad judgment or those who want good things for us?

This third question it's the most important of them all.
Why do we always listen to those that want us doing badly and not those who want the best for us?

Think about it and remember if justice doesn't forbid it to you, it means that you can do it. ***Do it!***

It must only matter to you what your bosses and direct family (spouse and/or children) think of you. The first ones because they condition you economically and the second ones, emotionally. These two groups are your economic and social wellbeing.

While you're in good terms with them, all will go great. Do you know what makes the world unstoppable? These two groups. Money and love, summed up they give power. Which, if you have emotional and financial intelligence, you won't be so vulnerable.

Retaking the subject of death, we all know people that have lost someone dear to them or even ourselves. When someone dear to us dies, we tend to think that life it's just rubbish, you only suffer and it's only two days, that's why you have to enjoy it. In no time you forget and you go back to the same routine.

People die to teach those of us who are alive that we must live as we feel and not as we are let to live. Death is there for you to live. Instead of focusing in the negative part, which is the absence of that person that you loved so much, focus yourself in the message that it has given you. Act and live as you want.

If you are a believer, that's great, that person will be with your God. The only inconvenient is the absence they left. Furthermore, your god is giving you a test, because I doubt he is against you, he knows you love him and he wants to help you. What he wants is for you to use your attitude to live as you want. That's why he has given you the capacity to choose and emotions. With these two capacities, your attitude is built, either good or bad one, you decide. God doesn't want your suffering or resignation. Pray as if all depends on him, but work as it all depends on you.

You're here passing by, take out of your head that you're immortal and that only the rest dies. If you're not a believer, that's great too. Reinforce your theories, whichever they are. As I mentioned before, you have the capacities to live as you want. The message is always the same: Make the best of the time you have left. While you're alive, everything is possible. Deprogram all of your irrational ideas and start again from zero. It's easier than it seems, read previous lines and remember the four laws of nature. Follow them literally.

When you have such a big problem that won't let you live in peace, think outside the box, and imagine you're someone else you're looking at yourself. What would you say to yourself? What advice would you give yourself to overcome these bad times?

Surely when a friend or relative has lost someone dear to them, you've given them one or another advice and you felt good when they listen to you and their mood change.
It may seem like a like, but problems from outside seem different, they get another perspective. They are more objective. Any problem you have, it's subjective. Make it come true, make it objective and you'll see it isn't that bad.

Most worries we have don't even get to happen. When you make them real, you'll find the solution. If you only digress, telling yourself I'd do this and that, you won't stop thinking and revolving around the subject. On the contrary, when you make them real and have them in front of you, you'll act to overcome that discomfort. But if even so you don't overcome it, imagine the worst scenario, what can happen? starting there you'll the solution.

Every now and then you have to go for a walk to the cemetery and and search for photos of people of our same age. Look at them and realize that they are not any more in this world and they can't do anything. But we are still here.
Let's be happy and let's do something we really like. Tomorrow, maybe it's you the one in the picture and I the one watching you.
After, basically, depression is thinking too often in the past and anxiety, thinking too much of the future. Starting there we could go deeper in the subject but I won't, there are many books and documentaries specialized in them.

Do this test: take a week thinking in how bad life is doing for you, you don't speak to your family, you're doing badly at work and when you go home, you feel lonely. You'll see how you'll end up. *Sad and melancholic!*

I'm going to tell you one last story so you see you aren't right when it comes to lack of time and the fact that having a daughter, you can't do nothing.

Laura: she is a single mother and she is also my neighbor. She is 32 and has an 8 year old daughter. When the girl was 3 years old, her husband died of cancer. Imagine the picture, being 27 and having a 3 year old daughter. She worked in a coffee shop and earned the minimum wage. She got information about the helped gave out by the estate for these kind of situations and thanks to them she could move on.

After 8 months she saw that wasn't a life, with the salary she earned she couldn't afford to satisfy her whims or buy anything else but that was necessary to survive. She was happy but she wanted a better lifestyle. She knew more than enough of my theories about economy and happiness but she never practiced them. Instead, her husband practiced some of them, like saving each month the 20% of your income. Thanks to those savings, he had 17.000 € on his bank account.

She asked her boss for a raise and he denied it. Then, she asked what could she do to earn more money without having to work extra hours, she was already working 10 hours daily and only one free day a week, she also wanted to have time to be with her daughter. She didn't like the idea of quitting her job because they were a reputable company, it was close to her house and she had great work companions.

The answer her boss gave her was that he had a vacancy for an accounting assistant. The monthly quotas were of 100€. She knew that if she used the money of her husband's bank account, in no time she wouldn't have anything. Once you start taking the money out, you don't stop. She came to me to teach her about emotional and financial intelligence so she could pay out her studies.

I helped her delighter, after ten months of careful study, she acquired the basic and necessary to enter the world of finances. She invested 16.000€ in a product that reported her earnings of 9% annually. That was around 1.440 € a year and divided in 12 months, that's 120 € a month. Now she had the money to pay her studies.

After a year studying, she got a degree that credited her as an accounting assistant and she took the vacancy her boss was offering her. Thanks to her steel attitude and the desire to overcome obstacles, she moved forward in life and lives the life she wants.
When your world is crumbling down, you only have two choices: resign or fight. While all went good for her she didn't need to earn more or change job.

The husband earned good money, he had free weekends and he could stay with their daughter. As a result of his death she had to wake up. Now she works 8 hours daily, she has free weekends, to be with her daughter and her salary has increased. She made of her adversity an opportunity to improve. It would have been easier to remain in that situation, complaining of her misfortunes and blaming the bad luck and her boss for not raising her salary.

She dedicated time, money and effort to prepare her knowledge, emotionally and financially.

Now she tastes what she has harvested. She knew how to make of a bad situation a good occasion. We all can live the life we want, but not all are willing to what's required.

When you like to work, it doesn't matter the job you have. You'll always do it good and will.

But if you don't want to invest, I think it's perfect. If you're not going to complain and assume the consequences, it's a very respectable option and I am glad for your decision. There's many of you that do it. You settle for a comfortable life, renouncing to that which you desire for fear of making an effort. After that, you self-apologize, thinking: I'll do it later, when I have more time. When my son or daughter it's older and I have less expenses, when I earn more, when I retire, etc. Knowing it's not true, those are simply excuses. The best of all, are the advices you give others: live to the fullest, that life are only days. Don't leave for tomorrow, what you can do today and many similar things like that.

Do you know what the IPC is?

- Of course! It's the monthly raise of the cost of living.

- Let me explain how your life gets poorer year after year without you realizing it. We have seven years without a raise, without taking into account the social cuts, nonetheless, the IPC doesn't stop going up. We pay more for our house, insurance, food, transportation, etc. Calculate how your cost of living rises annually and you'll get scared.

- It's not such a big deal, now I calculate: my passive expenses monthly ascend to 950 €, if I sum up the IPC, that this year has been of a 2%, it's about 950x2%= 19 € monthly.

By the end of the year it's 19X12= 228 €. Well yeah, that's a lot. It's about the annual quota of insurance of my car.

- Seeing this, don't you want to invest, even though it's only to regain the IPC? If you're afraid of taking risks, there's lot of insurance products.

One advice I want to give you: have available in your checking account at least passive expenses for 5 months. The reason is really simple. If you go unemployed, at least you'll have time to look for one that you like. If you've got nothing saved, you'll settle for the first one that appears.

Until now I've spoken about investment and why do them. If you're going to invest, take into account that no one is going to give you euros for cents.

I've previously mentioned financial products are the ones that offer best performance. Don't expect to invest in deposits and obtain rentability in actions.

If at one point you doubt, take the contract and deliver it to a professional in the area to inform you. Don't sign any contract without reading the small letters and if you still aren't clear, neither. *You're not in a hurry!*

When you buy a new car, you take it to your trusted mechanic so he gives out his opinion, right? Well that's worth for any investment you do.

If you buy a house, you'll better be with a professional on the area and gives out his opinion about the status of this house and the building. We all have a friend or someone we know that's into construction.

Better pay a first draft to a professional, than regretting all of your life for a bad investment

If you're going to mortgage yourself, first of all, study the market and inform yourself of the average price of the zone where you want to buy. As soon as you know it, your goal will be to get a 20% discount. Start offering 40% less and on the base of negotiations, you'll get to a 20%. Surely at first the seller will feel offended for your offer, but they'll get used to and want to negotiate. He/She wants to sell and you want to buy.

In business as in life, you'll only obtain what you don't ask for

Why is it that when you go to the supermarket of your city or town you haggle the price and in the rest your buys, you don't? You ask for discounts in supermarkets, or at least, ask if there's one.

You get all the discount cards these offer you. Many times when you buy an electrical appliance, this leads to a discount. But if you don't ask for it, the seller won't apply it.

This advice it's worth for any buy you do: in your insurance company, in your phone company, in the interests of your bancary investments, in anything related to money.

Above all, don't confuse yourself, you're not begging for nothing. You're simply working in the so called law "offer/demand".

In this first part I've talked about what you can do to live as you want, now I'm going to talk about appearances.

Living as you would like to live, trying to taste those flavors you don't have in your life.

The external difference between both doesn't exist, but inside, it's abysmal.

It's not the same to get to your house and follow the same routine than take off your mask and assume your frustrations. Likewise, thinking continuously on the possibility of being discovered.

Second Part

I lead the life I'd I would like to live (Appearances).

Do you know for what and why someone puts up appearances?

The answer to, for what? - It's very simple. It's done to obtain some satisfaction. The answer to, why? - It's more delicate.

Here come in play frustrations, fears and unsatisfied desires. The will to satisfy them it's the motivation that promotes action.

Appearances: carnival holidays only last for a few days for a reason. If it lasted more it would be terrible for society, no one is who says they are, and it's their reason to exist. During a few days you can avoid your problems and live being whom you want to be. No one is going to judge you, these are days to put up appearances. Pretending something you're not is frequently a way to try to be outstanding for superficial things. You choose a mask to fool others and in the end, we believe it ourselves. People rather be in mode *seems to be,* than mode *Be.* This last one requires having.

First you gotta have to be, if you're classy, you'll be elegant. If you have charisma, you'll be empathic and nice. If you have money, you'll be rich, not backwards. This is why people get frustrated in the mode seems to be, they're empty of content, and it's all a facade.

Is the need to belong to a group or stereotype to form or maintain a minimum of interpersonal relationships. Deprivation of these relationships can be a cause of serious mental disorders. The problem is, that's not real, but imaginary. It's a self-imposed need and as such, it doesn't have any way of escape. In any basic need, once covered, the organism relaxes and keeps working.

Escape route: it's a mechanism to unburden. Imagine that you are in a traffic jam and you get late to work, you get angry and honk, just doing it relaxes you. It's your escape route. Here we enter in the acquisition of relaxing techniques to not honk and relax in some other way. Any basic need that comes up, has this way. That's why it's important to satisfy them. If you're careless, the organism gets sick. Anxiety and depression appear.

The real problem of pretending something we're not, is that there comes a moment that the organism believes it and turns the deficiencies of that need in the same symptoms of real ones. The sick person if they don't cover them. Mostly for anxiety, fear of being discovered and be who they actually are.

Stereotypes: images in our mind that reflect our tendencies to think that people or things belong to the same category share similar characteristics.
When we want to judge someone or we try to take out information at a glance, we use stereotypes. They make life simpler and make easier our reality, enabling interaction. Generally, it's erroneous, well you tend to put everyone in the same sack, we classify them in some group we have in our mind.

People in suit: it comes to mind a banker, business man, lawyer but never a butcher, builder or delivery man. Instead of asking, we suppose. We believe that everyone thinks the same. Like I believe that if I am wearing a suit I look like a banker, others will think the same as I. Which, if I want to be seen as a banker, I'll wear suit. That's where problems start, the mistake of our beliefs.
"Rational as well as irrationals"

Another discomfort related to assumptions, is when we do someone a favor and doesn't return it. We suppose they'll return it, for the simple fact that we would do it. But it doesn't have to be like that, favors are done for pleasure. If you're not going to enjoy, it's not a favor, it's an obligation. Which for the other person, returning the favor, can be an obligation and that's why they don't do it. If you want it back, ask.

Living from appearances, it's not living your own life

You pretend for two reasons:

1. To get a limited goal in time, like a job or a fling.

2. As a lifestyle, for feeling frustrated.

Surely in your environment you know someone or you are one of them. I don't know you dear reader. If it's your case and want to change, you're in luck. I leave some guidelines of behavior so you can understand why you do it and this way you may change, if you want it.

In the first reason, the motivation that pushes to act is to find the desired objective; it's the most common among us. Impressing our future bosses so they can hire us or that person we like. Once we get it, we relax and we show ourselves just the way we are, it makes no sense to go on with the farce.

The second reason it's prejudicial. There's nothing better than being surrounded of people whom we can be ourselves. Showing how we truly are and being accepted without any conditions. Being what we aren't and being liked by certain people, is living for them. For as much as we fool people, we can't fool ourselves and the inner discomfort will appear even though we're accepted by others. We are here to be happy and not to please others.

What really matters is to know that no one is better than us, no matter the fortune or whatever the job. Each one of us are an added value to the society.

The importance you can give to any object or situation, emotional or material it's going to depend always on the moment, situation and place that you are. In life nothing is forever, it all goes changing.

The base of happiness is doing what you want. Therefore, if you pretend, you should be happy. You're supposed to act for pleasure, you do what you want. Sadly is not always like that, sometimes is for jealousy. It's the worst way, you enter into a world full of frustrations.

But is an unnatural jealousy, you envy a form of social life, not someone in specific. We all feel jealousy at some point in our life, but in proportion it's good. It's good for us as a motivation to reach the same things that our neighbor has, but without taking it away from him or underestimate it. It will make us think, what can I do to get where he has gotten?

In the case of someone that pretends it's more delicate, he envies a stereotype, which is already something subjective.
Being millionaire it's not the same to everyone; neither it's being famous, a recognized writer, soccer player, business man with success or an actor. Even worst, we know rich and humble people and they don't go around showing their economic power.

In this aspect the so called irrational ideas come in play: it all should be like that, I must go to that party even though I don't want to, I can't change my opinion even though I want to, everyone must love me, people should trust in the strongest, we must take care of others, you're worth what you have, people like you out of interest, etc.

These are ideas without a reasonable base, they're based in beliefs that we have since we were little and we hold on to them to predict facts. We associate ideas with events.

For example: the phone rings very late at night and a big tragedy comes to your mind.

Continuing with appearances, the real me with the ideal mea comes in conflict. It's the difference between what we are and we would like to be. The more distance there is between both, the more you'll want to pretend.

Real me: how we see ourselves, our self-perception. Above all we see the lacks we have and we don't see the virtues, we leave these to others.

Ideal me: includes all of our aspirations: being rich, famous, tall, small, handsome, athlete, muscular, intelligent, successful, etc…

I'm rich then I'm handsome and as such they'll love me. I'm famous and I'll be in the media and I'll become a millionaire. The fear of not being liked by others or to be rejected makes me behave in a different way than I am in reality. I think if I behave like others expect from me, I'll be liked more, I'll be more popular, I'll get more things, etc.

It shows a high grade of superficiality, lack of identity and self-esteem. It's a huge sign of dissatisfaction with oneself, which implies loss of self-identity. You don't know who you are and what you want in life. It's distortion of reality. One thing it's what you want it to be and another, what it really is. Not by being rich, you'll be handsome or nice, but if this is your reality, it's what you'll look for.

This person has a great feeling inferiority and low self-esteem. Constantly they criticize themselves; they are also, jealous, greedy and lazy.

They are jealous because they want the life other has and they feel unhappy with their own, they don't value what they have. They're greedy because they feel empty and must fill that space; in their eagerness to lead that way of life they accumulate many debts. They're lazy because they want to live the life of others but without making the effort it demands, they want another of life that isn't theirs because they have low self-esteem and think that way they'll be happy, without realizing that happiness comes from inside ourselves. The stereotype that they have created themselves is their ideal of life.

Low self-esteem: they feel lonely or rejected and they made up a social character with these features they desire and think they're not going to be rejected. Watching the success of that person they think if they're the same, they'll also attract fortune and wellbeing this person attracts. They want in a forced way to belong to a certain group, doing everything possible in looking in looking like members of the group, to be accepted. Even in occasions the jealous person has a higher social status than the one they're jealous of or more possessions. With this it's shown that flattery received as well as possessions, if you don't have a good self-esteem, it's worthless.

I give you some guidelines to rise up your self-esteem:

- Don't compare yourself to anyone, (you're not better or worst).
- Remember the happy moments of your daily life.
- Work out, (3-5 times a week).
- Don't take anything personal, you're not that important. Walk straight and with a steady step and when you shake someone's hand, do it with force *"strong and short"*.

The fact of going straight and shake hands firmly, it shows security and you reflect security in yourself. People see what you reflect.

If you have low self-esteem, try this guidelines for 21 days and I assure you it will rise. Now, don't stop after a week, saying it doesn't work. It would be like saying that you're studying a foreign language and the next week you quit because you can't speak it. After 21 days, you build a habit and after 3 months, it becomes regular. (Your new way of thinking and perceiving the daily happenings).

Happiness isn't achieved with what you have, but, making the best of what you have

For as many objects that you accumulate, if you don't enjoy them, they're worthless. Spend more money in emotional experiences and less in material objects. In time, objects lose value, instead emotional experiences; earn more value (think of your childhood, either good or bad). Create your personality with these last two. Don't forget what you are, what you are living now.

Do you want to suffer; depression, anxiety or none of these two?

Is like a builder that goes to work in a suit, thinking that when he is seen around town, people will think he is a classy man. When actually, class is inside. At the same time, many people that go with a suit, would want to go without it, but, because the work they do, that have to wear it. At any moment they think that, that's what makes them classy people, they don't even consider it. It's the stereotype of the person that pretends it. Before pretending something you're not, ask yourself, what do you want to achieve?

- their fortune
- their fame
- their friends
- their class

But above all ask yourself: for what?

The happiness of the person or stereotype which you're trying to imitate it's inside the person and it reflects in their interior, not backwards.

To feel good with yourself you need to be listened to, pay you attention and be well with you. The feeling of inferiority is such and loneliness that if you don't fill it faking it, you can't handle it. It's like a child that disguises himself of superman thinking like that he will be invincible and attract all the girls. During some time it feels great. This happens to the person that pretends something they're not. While the farce lasts, they feel good with themselves, they believe others see them as they see themselves. Let me put you the example of the politician so you understand it better:

The Politician: these are two friends that show themselves on the regional elections. For one, being a politician is: stealing, lying and placing friends in important positions.

For the other is: governing for the people, so they have a healthy wellbeing. It depends on who wins the elections, the people will go one way or the other.

Also it happens with the forces of order, you'll find with really nice and kind agents and even so, sometimes with borders, conceited and arrogant. That's why, for some, being an agent means behaving with education with the citizen and helping them in everything possible, instead for others it means, being oppressors and humiliating them.

They don't do it with bad intentions or consciously, because later, they go on the streets without the uniform and are exemplary citizens, it's the concept they have of this role.

They only look at the facade in the outside. They've got the belief that everything else comes along, like a magnet. The agent that behaves with dignity, and has the belief that if he treats people well, they will respond back in the same way and puts himself in his place. He also likes to be treated right.

The one that behaves in a repressive and humiliating way has the belief that it's the only way to make him respected. When someone interacts with him, he doesn't know any other way to answer but taking orders. He usually has a profile of someone submissive, obedient and doesn't know how to say no, well he is incapable of defying anyone. In consequence, he places his hostility towards others, believing himself superior to them. It's a person totally insecure and with the role of authority, he is full of himself.

This example can be extrapolated to any figure of power; it's more valued the meaning of the stereotype than the person.

Watch and see that other people are happy leading that life, but they don't see what they have done to get there and obtain that result. In occasions if he knows it, but don't want to make the necessary effort to achieve it. To be rich and maintain the fortune or raise it up, economy and investments must be understood. If they only copy the facade, the day they have to talk of a related subject, you'll unmask them.

They look for the fast way to success and that wears you out emotionally in a destructive way. Depression and anxiety are very related with the *I want* and *I can't*. Taking short cuts it's not always good and even less acquiring culture.

<u>Glory it's a pile of well invested hours</u>

Stereotypes are different in each country and culture. A very clear example: **A young man in his 20's and his sport car:** imagine he is going to go around the world in his car and you find him in any European city, you'll think he is just a spoiled kid or a yuppie.

Instead, if you find him in any Latin American city, you'll think he is a drug dealer. You'll treat him differently according to the place you find him and he will act the same way with you. We behave according to how we are treated, we're our own reflection, we act according to our beliefs.

Do the test: today when you go out to the street and you get crossed by people, don't say hi or smile, oddly, they won't smile or say hi to you back. You're reflecting your discomfort in your behavior, when someone hurts you or smiles at you, they do it according to their emotional state. This wouldn't have to affect you at all. It's their problem if they have a bad day.

If you want people to smile and be kind to you, do that with others. Project happiness, harmony and happiness. But don't misunderstand me, if they hurt you, defend yourself.

What I mean, is that once you're defined, you go back to your previous state of tranquility, don't allow someone else's bad humor ruin your inner peace and even less, your day.

On being young and with a sport car, it's shown that not for everyone is the same, some would want to be seen as the most powerful drug dealer of their city and others, as the richest.

I've remembered a guy I met in New York. I went to an economy seminar on Wall Street and we met in the coffee shop in front of it. The guy had won a trip of five days, with all expenses paid.

The jealous neighbor: this guy worked in his brother's mechanic workshop, he took care of changing tires and he earned his life in a good way but he was jealous of his neighbor, whom was always wearing trendy suits, he drove a Porsche and always ate out. Instead of asking him what he did to live that kind of life, he started copying him. He got indebted with a sport car and took his credit cards to the limit, eating in luxurious restaurants and going to the same places as his neighbor.

On one occasion they met in a club and they started talking, the rich neighbor asked him what he did for a living and he answered that he was a mechanic, the amazed neighbor answers:

- Wow! You must earn a lot to have a sport car.
- Yes, actually I am the owner and I can't complaint, and what do you do for a living?
- Nothing, I don't work, my parents have business and we live from rents. I spent the day from here and there. I am really glad for your business and I hope it all keeps going as well as now, he answers again while he goes up in his brand new Porsche.

If he would have asked instead of copy, he wouldn't be indebted living the life he can't afford and lying.

My friend, ask and don't copy. When you feel jealous of someone, it's better to be embarrassed for a few seconds for asking, than being in discomfort many days for not doing it.

In the case of this guy, he thought that pretending to be a yuppie; he was going to have more dates, seen better by the rest of the community and being accepted in the circle of friends of his neighbor. He felt alone and needed company in any way. He had the idea that his neighbors underestimated him for getting home each day with his face and hands full of grease. He felt inferior to them without any real reason.

He was complexed and had low self-esteem, he underestimated himself. He felt less than others and thought that he was unable to do nothing being himself. In the workshop, his mates bully him for being too clumsy. He had the work because he needed it, he didn't like it and gave him his desired life.

When he finished his studies it was the first job he got. That's why it's important to do what you like.

With the conduct of pretending to be something he's not, he got the exact opposite; his community was wondering if he had won the lottery or something like that. They didn't understood how a salary of a tires changer could afford such lifestyle. But the best in this story is that his neighbors respected him a lot, even though he was full of grease, he didn't stain the wall or elevator. To thank him for the detail of not tarnishing the building they were going to prepare a surprise party for his next birthday.

As I've already mentioned before: we suppose instead of asking.

If you're jealous of your friend from work, ask him what he's done to get that role you would want to occupy. Maybe you won't like his answer. Maybe he got there in some ways you may not like. You have certain values and principles and you respect them to the fullest.
      He could have also, gotten there studying after work, while you to the bar or gym, he stays home or in an academy studying. If you think about it and ask him how he's gotten there, may be so much effort doesn't compensate you and you quit, What's sure, is that the feeling of jealousy will banish, well you'll already know what to do to reach that position.

Unless, you're one of those that want the prize without doing the necessary effort, then you're doomed to frustration and to general discomfort. Nothing is going to satisfy your thirst of having what you can't.

The jealous person doesn't know what he wants until he sees what other has

In regards of the behavior towards others, I expose one interesting effect, capable of conditioning your way of acting. It's called:

Self-fulfilled prophecy or Pygmalion effect: it's produced when people maintain certain expectations of you and you change your conduct and behavior according to expectations.

I'll explain it to you in another way so you can understand it better: you're in class and the professor treats as dumb and useless the two or three in the bottom of the row. These students will end up behaving as such, to please the professor. They'll acquire the role of dumb and useless.
With this example I want you to understand, that if your parents or friends have always treated you like a clown or a fool or on the contrary, like the smartest and most sure of himself. Every time you see them, in front of them you'll behave in the same way.
The bad thing of this behavior is that it can be generalize to any situation. You'll behave according to what others expect of you.

So it's clear for you, **I'll tell you the case of Lucía:** she's a 57 year old full-fledged woman, with three kids and happily married. She's owner of an agency in Alicante. We met in Lisbon, in a coffee shop near the tower of Belém. Her case was somewhat peculiar. Every time she heard of some friend's disgrace, she broke down in tears. She spend two or three days with huge discomfort, headache and anxiety. Talking to her, I saw her behavior was due to her crying because she thought it was the right thing to do.

She thought it was what others expected of her. To feel bad for a few days. The mind is so powerful it can create diseases out of nowhere, only thinking you're sick, you can get sick.

Well, Lucía, when she was 5 she lost her older brother. She barely cried, she was too little to realize what happened. He mother, was too sensitive, she didn't understood the behavior of her daughter and taught her that when someone dies or is doing bad, the common thing to do is get sick of sadness and cry for them.

Circumstances in life made that in less than 4 years, lost three family friends. Obeying the mother, she acquire the habit of getting sick and have a bad time when misfortunes occur. In time she has develop it, while reading the newspaper or watching the news, she gets sick of sadness.

Taking that into account, if you get together with positive and joyful people, they're going to appreciate you for what you are and they'll motivate you in everything you want to do. Since they're going to have good expectations about you, without realizing it you'll give out the best of you. With this environment so cozy and motivating, you'll make a bigger effort, because they'll push you to do it. Any goal you put yourself is a lot easier to achieve, that's why it's important.

If in school or at work you're being harassed, (bullying), but out of there you have positive emotions and you feel appreciated and protected by others, it will be like a mattress, it cushions the hit. You'll notice that you've been hit but it won't affect your conduct in the least. Every time that you go back to school or work, you'll do it with renewed energies and being sure of yourself.

Now that you've finish reading the book, you must have realized the importance to have assets. Alongside your salary you must always have another ways of income.

<u>Your money has to work for you!</u>

In regards of appearances, if you know someone like that or you are one of them, you already know the reasons of this behavior. If you don't know who you are, you won't know what to do. You'll wander around without knowing where to go, today you imitate someone and tomorrow another and you'll never be satisfied or fulfilled.

<u>You want that which you desire, but you don't want to make the effort to get it</u>

Notes from the author: low self-esteem it's destructive and distorts the perception of your reality. That's why it's important to spoil yourself, give yourself whims and remember daily the good things that happen to you.

www.ingramcontent.com/pod-product-compliance
Lightning Source LLC
Chambersburg PA
CBHW071725040426
42446CB00011B/2221